Whistles Round the Bend

BOOKS BY PHIL AULT

Whistles Round the Bend
By the Seat of Their Pants
"All Aboard!"
Wires West
These Are the Great Lakes
This Is the Desert
Wonders of the Mosquito World

Whistles Round
the Bend

TRAVEL ON AMERICA'S WATERWAYS

BY PHIL AULT

Illustrated with photographs, old prints, and maps

Dodd, Mead & Company · New York

Copyright © 1982 by Phillip H. Ault
All rights reserved
No part of this book may be reproduced in any form
    without permission in writing from the publisher
Printed in the United States of America

1   2   3   4   5   6   7   8   9   10

Library of Congress Cataloging in Publication Data

Ault, Phillip H., date
    Whistles round the bend.

    Bibliography: p.
    Includes index.
    Summary: Traces the history of travel on
America's rivers, the Great Lakes, and the Erie
Canal and spotlights the vehicles used.
    1. Inland navigation—United States—History.
2. Inland water transportation—United States—
History. [1. Inland water transportation—History.
2. Steamboats] I. Title.
HE627.A9   386'.0973   81-19574
ISBN 0-396-08036-7   AACR2

For MASSI, who sailed a Norwegian ship
through the Great Lakes many years ago

Contents

The luxurious tourist steamboat the Mississippi Queen

CHAPTER ONE

Steamboat A-comin'!

HERE she comes now. Nosing slowly upstream against the current, her low, rounded prow cutting through the restless patterns of ripples and eddies that mottle the surface of the Mississippi River, the *Mississippi Queen* appears around a bend. Her whistle bellows a thunderous blast. Tourists lean over her hurricane deck as she glides under an arching bridge and turns in toward anchorage at the levee that protects the historic city of Vicksburg, Mississippi.

From the top of a cliff far above the east bank of the river, just south of the city, spectators peer at her along the barrel of a Confederate Army cannon, unfired for more than a hundred years. Like a multi-tiered white wedding cake, pushed along by a gigantic red stern paddle wheel, the *Mississippi Queen* moves across the gun's line of fire, trailed by a wake of foam.

"*Boom!*" shouts a boy behind the artillery piece, pretending he is a soldier.

But the luxurious modern riverboat coasts serenely into the wharf. Crew and passengers are unaware that, if the clock had been turned back into another century, their vessel might have been battered by shells from that unseen cannon. Other boats did fall prey to it one fiery night in the early 1860s when North and South fought in deadly combat to control this mightiest of America's water highways.

Vicksburg! The name recalls one of the crucial battles of the Civil War—and much more, too. It stirs memories of life in the early days of our country when the only "roads" through the wilderness were rutted trails, often bogged down in mud, and our forefathers traveled as much as they could on the rivers. Where no navigable rivers existed, they built the Erie Canal and other man-made waterways to help move the mass of new settlers westward. Large portions of the eastern half of the country were covered with forest, gloomy and difficult to penetrate with wagon roads. Travel by foot or horse was slow and often perilous. Towns like Vicksburg came into existence at convenient points along the rivers and canals, as resting places for travelers and as loading points for the produce of the farms the settlers had carved out of the wild land.

The determined bands of newcomers who penetrated into the vast empty regions of the United States during the 1800s pushed the frontier farther and farther to the west. As much as possible, the frontier followed the streams. Most of America's great inland

Surrounded by mist that obscures the banks of the Mississippi River, the Mississippi Queen *noses ashore at a muddy landing place much as pioneer steamboats did 150 years earlier.*

This Confederate cannon on the bluffs overlooking Vicksburg, Mississippi, was one of those that fired on General Grant's Union steamboats as they sailed past the city's defenses in 1863.

cities were created on the edge of water, either rivers and canals or the Great Lakes. These lakes, too, were part of the water route to the West.

When settlers reached the Southwest and the Far West, they found more rivers. Quickly they put them to use. Steamboats poked their way inland up the Columbia and the Sacramento from the Pacific Ocean. They struggled up the Colorado River from the Gulf of California through torrid, barren desert, often running aground. Adventurous Texans took steamboats up the Brazos and the Rio Grande. In fact, wherever a river flowed more than two feet deep, steamboatmen tried to sail their almost flat-bottomed craft.

"All I need to keep this boat afloat is a heavy dew," some of them claimed.

As the *Mississippi Queen* sidled up to the Vicksburg wharf, crewmen pushed out gangplanks. Tourists came ashore in flocks, carrying cameras, many of the women and men wearing shorts. Guides organized them in groups and drove them up the bluffs into the center of the city on a sight-seeing tour.

The *Mississippi Queen* and her older, smaller sister ship, the *Delta Queen*, are the only two boats left on the Mississippi River that make overnight trips carrying passengers. The steamboats that once took passengers on overnight excursion trips along the seacoasts are gone, too, as are the Great Lakes steamers. The *Queens* cater to tourists who want to get a taste of how life used to be on the rivers, not to travelers like their great-grandparents who used the boats because they were the fastest and most comfortable way to move from city to city.

Indeed, the recently constructed, all-steel *Mississippi Queen* resembles an old-time steamboat, even the most elaborate river packet of early days, about as much as a sleek modern motel on an interstate highway does an aged group of tourist cabins on a minor road. The *Queen*'s cabins are air-conditioned; there are elevators between decks, a plate-glass wall two stories high at the stern, and a swimming pool. The *Queen* is propelled by diesel engines, instead of the clanking steam engines into whose boilers gangs of deck hands constantly threw wood.

How different the Vicksburg levee was in the middle of the nineteenth century when the steamboat was king!

Visualize a summer day in the mid-1850s, if you can: Tall wooden steamboats are tied side by side at the wharf. Towering iron smokestacks rise in pairs above each boat, their flaring tops adorned with frilly patterns, giving the impression of a thicket of huge metal posts. Bales of cotton stacked high on the levee are being loaded by singing gangs of roustabouts onto the deck of a steamer headed downriver to market at New Orleans. The tune of a harmonica drifts from behind the bales.

Women in billowing dresses that almost sweep the ground step daintily along the levee toward the gangplank of another boat preparing to depart. They carry parasols to protect themselves from the hot Southern sun. Men lift trunks and carpetbags to the boat's low main deck from horse-drawn wagons standing alongside. With those dresses, women needed bulky luggage!

From high above in the glass-enclosed pilothouse the captain watches the last-minute bustle. He signals and the steamboat's warning bell clangs. A steward bangs a Chinese gong, shouting, "All that aren't going, please get ashore!"

The plank is pulled in. A strip of water appears between the hull and the shore as the vessel turns out into the stream. Plumes of black smoke sprinkled with sparks pour from its stacks; the deck vibrates as the engines settle into a rhythmic sound, something like *chukety pow, chukety pow, chukety pow.* Pushed by the paddle wheels churning the water at its sides, the boat points its bow upstream. To where: Memphis, St. Louis, or perhaps up the Ohio River all the way to Cincinnati?

That scene has vanished into the haze of time. But the river still rolls along, days without end, draining the vast central regions of the United States just as it has since taking its present form when the last massive ice cap melted and withdrew northward about thirty thousand years ago.

The Mississippi River and its tributaries drain two-fifths of the United States. A map of their waters resembles a spreading tree: the base of the trunk at the Gulf of Mexico below New Orleans, its topmost branch reaching 2350 miles up to the river's source at Lake Itasca, in northwestern Minnesota. One giant branch, the Ohio River, points east from the southern tip of Illinois, all the way into the Appalachian Mountains that form the barrier behind the Atlantic Ocean coast. Above St. Louis, Missouri, the muddy Missouri River flows in from the northwest on a meandering course across the Plains from the distant Rocky Mountains. Steamboaters maneuvered their vessels along nearly nine thousand miles of the Mississippi River system, up side streams so shallow that the boats could stay afloat only in the months of heavy rain and runoff from melting snow.

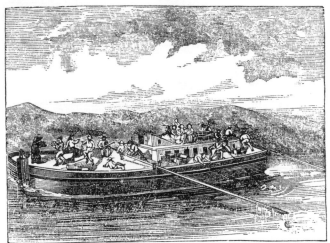

Early modes of travel on America's waterways—by canoe, keelboat, and flatboat

The heights of Vicksburg provided a splendid place from which to watch the cavalcade of adventurers, immigrants, and other travelers who were swept down by the Mississippi's current, and sometimes fought their way back upstream. The Indians in their canoes came first. For them, the Mississippi and other rivers formed watery "highways" long before the first white settlers reached American soil from Europe. Often covering long distances, native paddlers maneuvered their frail birchbark craft up and down the streams and along the shores of the Great Lakes.

Two French explorers, Father Jacques Marquette and Louis Joliet, paddled down to the mouth of the Arkansas River in 1673, not quite as far as Vicksburg. In the spring of 1682, Robert Cavelier, Sieur de la Salle, most far-ranging of the French explorers, led his flotilla of canoes down to the river's mouth. There he raised the flag of France and grandiosely claimed the entire Mississippi valley for that country, naming it Louisiana for his king.

After the Revolutionary War, Americans eager to establish homes in the wild, beckoning interior of their new country floated down the Ohio River in makeshift rafts and flatboats hewn from logs. They called rafts that used oars on each side "broadhorns." Some traveled on bullboats, which consisted of buffalo hides stretched over a sapling frame to form an enormous oval basket twenty-five feet long and twelve feet wide. The settlers broke ground for farms along the riverbanks in what are now Ohio, Kentucky, Indiana, and Illinois. Because hauling the produce of their fields upstream to sell was extremely difficult, many took it instead down the Mississippi to New Orleans.

Soon came the keelboats, and after them the steamboats.

Primitive as they seem to us, the keelboats ruled the big rivers from the 1790s until about 1820. A keelboat was approximately seventy feet long, built of rough lumber. Unlike the flatboat, it had a pointed nose and stern. Its deck was roofed over, and it had a mast for a sail. The keelboat's great advantage was that it could go upstream, which rafts and flatboats could not.

The trip upstream was accomplished by sheer muscle power.

A flatboat on its one-way trip down the Mississippi

Cleated runways a foot or two wide were built along both sides of
the keelboat. Pairs of men stood near the bow on each side, jabbed
twelve-foot poles into the river bottom, then jogged toward the
stern, pushing the boat forward. Sometimes they used oars, or they
grabbed branches of bushes and low trees on shore and pulled the
boat ahead. This was called "bushwhacking." Another method of
moving against the current was to tie one end of a thousand-foot
rope high on the mast; crew members walking along the shore
dragged the other end. Keelboats averaged about one mile an hour
upstream, fifteen miles a day. Crawling hundreds of miles up the
Mississippi in that manner required great endurance, so it isn't surprising that keelboatmen were a rough, boisterous lot. They fought
often, drank heavily, and boasted that they were "half horse, half
alligator."

Most famous, or infamous, of the keelboatmen was big-talking, blustering, brawling Mike Fink, whose exploits along the Mississippi and the Missouri have become bigger-than-life legends. Mike often bragged about how well he could shoot his frontier rifle. One day he and a friend named Carpenter exchanged dares to shoot a can from the other man's head. Carpenter shot first, and his bullet knocked the can from Fink's head, grazing his skull. When Fink's turn came, he fired and killed Carpenter. Another man then killed Mike Fink in revenge. This happened at Fort Henry, at the mouth of the Yellowstone River.

Such were the ways of the keelboaters.

Had the citizens of Vicksburg known who was aboard a flatboat that floated past their town in the spring of 1828, and what he would mean to them in the future, they would have paid more attention. It was just another clumsy craft of poplar logs lashed together, with a rough-hewn shelter on top and long steering oars front and back. Scores of such vessels drifted downriver every week. The flatboat was loaded with pork, flour, bacon, and corn.

If anyone had asked his name, the gawky woodsman who tugged on the front oar would have replied, "Abe. Abe Lincoln." At nineteen, he was making his first trip away from the log cabins where he grew up in Kentucky and southern Indiana. A merchant, James Gentry, had hired Abe to help his son maneuver the flatboat loaded

The keelboat was designed to make the return trip upstream.

with produce more than a thousand miles down the Ohio and Mississippi to New Orleans. They required two months to make the trip around scores of river bends, through swirling eddies, over sandbars, and past half-sunken trees that lurked in the water, ready to rip the bottom from a passing craft. Abe earned eight dollars a month and saw with his own eyes how others lived. He watched slaves being sold, and the sight appalled him.

Thirty-five years later the same lanky man, now President Abraham Lincoln, ordered his Union Army generals to capture Vicksburg from the Confederate Army and open the entire Mississippi River to Northern shipping. Memories of his youthful trip and the hilly contours around the vital river port must have been strong in his mind as he studied plans for the attack.

Frequently during the Civil War, the generals moved their men by steamboat. Hundreds of soldiers could be jammed aboard vessels that had plied the rivers as ornate passenger steamers in peacetime. With some of their expensive furnishings removed, but

Old print shows Union gunboats attacking Fort Donelson on the Cumberland River in 1862. The gunboats were converted riverboats.

William Tecumseh Sherman, LEFT, *and Ulysses S. Grant*

with no protection from enemy fire, the boats became troop transports. Built entirely of wood, they were ripe targets for enemy shells and cannonballs.

Control of the Mississippi River was extremely important to both the North and the South, for movement of troops and supplies. Already holding the upper portion, the North gradually won command of the lower stretches of the river. In the middle stood Vicksburg, stubbornly blocking the way. This Confederate stronghold was deeply entrenched. The cannon on her cliffs commanded the river channel in front of the city. Confederate soldiers along the shore could rake the stream with rifle fire.

Early in 1863, General Ulysses S. Grant loaded his army aboard steamboats at Helena, Arkansas, and headed downstream toward Vicksburg in impressive array—sixty-seven steamboats in a line, protected by twenty Union gunboats.

The Union troops under Grant and General William Tecumseh Sherman attacked Vicksburg by land from the north. The stout Confederate defenses turned them back time after time. Grant then decided to strike from the south by ferrying his troops across the river to the west bank above the city and marching them down the sparsely populated west shore on the Louisiana side of the river, where they would be outside the range of Vicksburg's guns. They

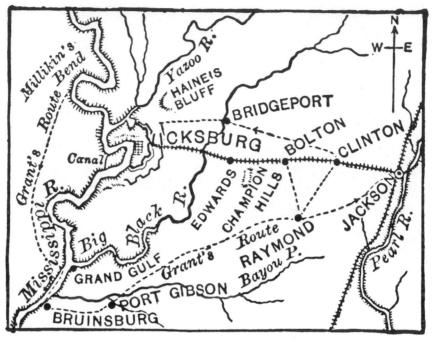

Grant's route in the attack on Vicksburg

would recross the river below the city, march back to the north, circle behind Vicksburg, and pin the Confederate forces against the east bank of the river.

But how could the Union army make the return crossing of the broad Mississippi from the west bank below Vicksburg? It must have steamboats there to transport men, animals, and supplies. Grant decided to gamble. He would send a convoy of empty passenger steamboats guarded by gunboats straight through the blockade—have them run past Vicksburg at night through the withering Confederate barrage he knew would be unleashed if the boats were detected.

The night of April 16, 1863, was clear but dark, without a moon. Not a light could be seen from the point above Vicksburg where General Grant stood outside his headquarters. Two hours before midnight, around the bend came a dim silhouette out in the river, drifting silently with the current toward the first Confederate gun emplacements. Then another, and another. The Union flotilla was on the move. Eleven boats in line two hundred yards apart were making the dash, including three army transports and another passenger boat whose prow had been rebuilt to form a pointed iron ram.

At the front was the gunboat *Benton*. The gunboats were stripped-down steamboats whose sides were covered with sloping walls of oak logs. Outside the logs was a one-inch layer of India rubber, and on top of that plates of iron. Sometimes gunboat commanders had the iron plates coated with tallow or grease, to make the enemy's cannonballs glance off more easily. The crews fired their guns through portholes in the armored sides that could be opened and closed.

With a tugboat lashed to her far side, the *Benton* slipped silently past the first Confederate guns without drawing fire. Then in the darkness came the sharp crack of rifle shots. Defending soldiers

Union gunboats under Confederate fire, Vicksburg, April 16, 1863

crouched along the Vicksburg levee peppered the *Benton* with bullets, most of which bounced off her slanted sides.

Confederate drummers beat the "long roll," calling the garrison to arms. Soon flashes blazed on the cliffs as the heavy guns thundered.

Suddenly the black midnight sky came alight. Confederate soldiers set fire to houses on both banks, and to barrels of tar they had placed in anticipation of the blockade-running attempt. Against the flames, vessels stood out in bold silhouette, giving the Confederate gunners splendid targets. The shots from their cannons battered the sides of the Union boats, sometimes breaking through the armor and logs into the crew areas.

As she passed the levee, the *Benton* boldly steered barely a hundred feet offshore, opened her portholes, and fired broadsides into the buildings of Vicksburg. Each of the following gunboats did the same.

Behind the gunboats came the troopships. Bales of cotton and sandbags stacked high on their decks were the only protection these flimsy wooden boats had against intense Confederate fire. An exploding shell ignited the *Henry Clay*'s cotton bale "armor," and in minutes the vessel was ablaze like a huge torch. All her crew except the pilot abandoned ship in rowboats. He tried bravely to save the boat single handed, until flames forced him to jump overboard. He grabbed a plank and floated to safety through chunks of blazing debris.

General Sherman, describing the battle later, said, "The roar of cannon, the bursting of shell, and finally the burning of the *Henry Clay*, drifting with the current, made up a picture of the terrible not often seen."

The Northern convoy got through, nevertheless—all but the *Henry Clay*. Although the vessels were pockmarked by gunfire and in some cases badly damaged, not a Union sailor was killed. Twelve were wounded.

Using the boats as ferries, General Grant as planned led his army back across the river below Vicksburg and around the the city. The

The Union fleet of passenger steamboats and gunboats runs past the Confederate blockade at Vicksburg under heavy cannon fire from shore, as depicted in this Currier and Ives print. The Benton *leads the way as the* Henry Clay *burns.*

besieged civilian inhabitants and the Confederate soldiers held on gallantly for weeks under incessant Northern bombardment as their food supplies dwindled until, half-starved, they surrendered on the Fourth of July. Once again the nation's greatest waterway was open to travel, and it never has been closed since. Only the perils of the river itself threatened the passing vessels.

CHAPTER TWO

Ahoy, Floating Dishpans!

WHEN young Mrs. Nicholas Roosevelt announced that she was going as a passenger aboard the *New Orleans*, the only woman passenger, on the first steamboat trip ever attempted down the Ohio and Mississippi rivers, she realized that it would be a risky adventure. She knew that she was going to have a baby in about a month, somewhere on the edge of the wilderness. That would be enough to scare off most women. She was aware that the flimsy, untested *New Orleans* might blow up or sink in the rapids it would encounter on the 2000-mile journey from Pittsburgh to New Orleans. Warnings by worried friends that Indians might attack the boat left her undaunted. But she never expected earthquakes, too.

In the fall of 1811, Lydia Roosevelt accompanied her husband on the voyage that revolutionized Western travel. (Everywhere west of the Appalachian Mountains was considered the West in those days.) Until then, every craft that had ever ventured onto those tricky waters had been propelled by wind or by the muscles of men—canoes, flatboats, keelboats, and other floating objects that made use of the current.

Mrs. Roosevelt didn't scare easily. After all, hadn't she made the same journey two years earlier as far as Natchez, Mississippi, on a flatboat, as a bride? Her honeymoon "cottage" had been a shack on the crude raft's deck. And hadn't she and Nicholas traveled the

Robert Fulton

final 268 miles to New Orleans from Natchez in a rowboat, taking nine days?

Although he was far away, back in New York, the man responsible for the Roosevelts' ventures into the wilderness was Robert Fulton, who is often credited with inventing the steamboat. That isn't quite accurate. Other men in the United States and England had built experimental boats, but Fulton was the first to put the principles of steam to practical use in a boat, his famous *Clermont*. Fulton was an artist from Pennsylvania who went to Paris to paint and, while there, became interested in engineering. He was building an experimental submarine in France when wealthy Robert Livingston, the American ambassador, convinced him to return to the United States and build a steamboat. Fulton was confident that he knew how.

The painter-turned-boatbuilder had a small steam engine shipped to New York from England. He designed a hull similar to those of fast ocean sailing ships, extending seven feet deep under the water's surface. In this hold he placed the engine, and on the deck he constructed two masts for sails, as reserve power. Smoke emerged from a single stack near the forward mast. From each side of the hull extended a primitive paddle wheel with no covering over its blades. The *Clermont* was 130 feet long and 16 feet wide.

New Yorkers who watched the boat under construction called it "Fulton's Folly." They simply couldn't believe that a steamboat would work.

Fulton showed them it would and became famous. On August 17, 1807, he invited forty friends and relatives aboard for a trial trip from New York up the Hudson River to Albany. Everyone was anxious, including Fulton, and some were outright frightened. The *Clermont* started proudly enough, but after a short distance stopped dead in the water. Murmurs of "I told you so!" and "I knew it would never work" rose among the guests.

Fulton described the crisis later: "I elevated myself upon a platform and addressed the assembly. I stated that I did not know what was the matter, but if they would be quiet and indulge me for half an hour, I would either go on or abandon the voyage for that time."

Climbing down into the hold, he tinkered with the engine, made an adjustment or two, and, to his relief, the *Clermont* began moving through the water again.

Fulton felt triumphant. As for his dubious guests, he reported later, "All were still incredulous. None seemed willing to trust the evidence of their own senses."

Thereafter, the *Clermont* behaved splendidly. It chugged the 150 miles up to Albany in thirty-two hours, averaging about five miles an hour against the current. Suddenly, instead of being a foolish dabbler in the eyes of many, Fulton was a hero. With small cabins added, the *Clermont* began runs up and down the Hudson, the start of passenger boat service on that river that lasted more than 130 years.

Livingston and Fulton were shrewd businessmen, too. Somehow they obtained from the state of New York exclusive rights to run their boats on its rivers. They wangled the same arrangement in Louisiana, at the lower end of the Mississippi River. All they needed to profit from this monopoly was to get steamboat service started on the Mississippi. That is where the Roosevelts entered the picture. First Livingston and Fulton sent them on the flatboat trip, to get an idea of the problems involved. Then they put up money for

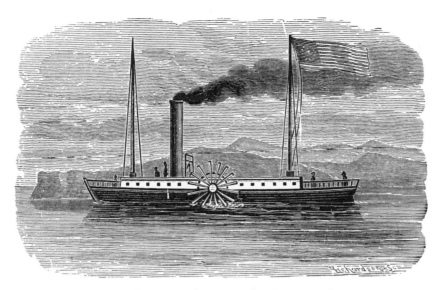

Robert Fulton's Clermont, *the first steamboat*

construction of the *New Orleans* at Pittsburgh under Roosevelt's supervision.

The *New Orleans* was a first cousin of the *Clermont*. Fulton designed the Mississippi steamer to resemble the *Clermont*, except that it was five feet deep instead of seven. It, too, had an engine imported from England, and sails. Fulton sent fifty mechanics from New York to help with the shipbuilding.

At first the trip went smoothly for the Roosevelts and the *New Orleans* crew. The Roosevelts' huge Newfoundland dog, Tiger, ran up and down the deck, barking at animals along the forested shore. Wherever there was a village, the inhabitants stopped work to stare in surprise at the plume of black smoke rising from the first steamboat they had ever seen. At Cincinnati, the mayor gave a welcoming speech.

When the *New Orleans* reached Louisville, trouble began. The fundamental mistake Fulton had made in designing the boat for western river travel became apparent: The boat's bottom sat too low in the water for rivers full of sandbars, shoals, and rapids. The

Hudson was a deep-water river, but the Ohio and most of the Mississippi were not. Just below Louisville is a rocky place known as the Falls of the Ohio, where the river drops twenty-four feet in three miles over a series of limestone ledges. Until winter rains raised the level of the river, the *New Orleans* could proceed no farther. While the party waited for the river to rise, Mrs. Roosevelt had her baby in the ladies' cabin at the rear of the boat.

With a tiny infant as an additional passenger, the captain of the *New Orleans* decided on the last day of November to make a run for it. Test measurements showed that if he steered the vessel in precisely the right place, there would be clearance of five inches between the bottom of its hull and the menacing rocks. Puffing smoke and weaving through the white water channel, the *New Orleans* slipped through safely and anchored in the river below. Everyone except the baby rejoiced. It cried.

Then a strange thing happened. The boat began to gyrate in the water, bouncing up and down and twisting around. Pots and pans in the galley shook, as though in an ocean storm. An earthquake!

The *New Orleans* had been caught in what may have been the worst series of earthquakes ever to strike the United States. Geologists call them the New Madrid Earthquakes, after the Missouri town on the Mississippi River that was the hardest hit of the settlements in the earthquake area. Earth tremors lasted for three months, some of them so severe that sections of land along the Mississippi rose or fell as much as twenty feet. Two large lakes were created, one on each side of the river.

There was nothing better for the *New Orleans* to do but steam ahead, past crumbling riverbanks that swept away landmarks the pilots had used to find the channel.

Mrs. Roosevelt wrote later, "No one seemed disposed to talk, and when there was any conversation, it was carried on in whispers almost. Tiger who appeared alone, to be aware of the earthquake while the vessel was in motion, prowled about, moaning and groaning."

The New Orleans, *designed by Robert Fulton and built at Pittsburgh. In her, the Nicholas Roosevelts made the first steamboat trip down the Ohio and Mississippi rivers to New Orleans. Their baby was born aboard in the ladies' cabin.*

Soon a new danger seemed to threaten the vessel. A canoe filled with Indians came out from the shore one day; those on the *New Orleans* feared they were about to be attacked by savages. Quite possibly the Indians weren't belligerent but were only frightened and baffled by the combination of earthquakes, which are extremely rare in that region, and the appearance of the "fire canoe," spitting smoke and sparks. The *New Orleans* crew, whose nerves were on edge, didn't wait to find out; they turned on full speed and outdistanced the canoe.

Everybody was tense. That night Roosevelt heard feet rushing along the deck. His first thought was, "Indian attack!" He jumped from bed and ran onto the deck, brandishing a sword to repel the attackers. But it wasn't an Indian raid. It was something almost as bad. The boat was on fire. Most of the forward cabin was destroyed before the flames were extinguished.

The New Orleans *was caught in the terrible series of earthquakes and floods that centered on New Madrid, Missouri, in 1811. The old print shows a flood of a later date at Cairo, Ohio. Note the floating snags.*

From then on, the trip, as the *New Orleans* turned from the Ohio into the Mississippi and down that combined stream, was a nightmare. When the vessel put in at New Madrid, frightened residents asked to be taken aboard and carried away from the area, but the boat had neither space nor food for them. Day after day the earth trembled. The quakes jarred hundreds of sunken trees to the surface, where their branches and trunks were a constant threat to the boat, and caused floods as well. One night the *New Orleans* was tied up to a small island; when daylight came, the crew discovered that the island had vanished.

"I lived in constant fright unable to sleep or sew or read," Mrs. Roosevelt reported.

Despite these perils, eventually the *New Orleans* arrived in her namesake city, more than three months after leaving Pittsburgh. The boat had accomplished her mission of bringing steamboat travel to the great inland river system and was welcomed joyously at the Louisiana port. After a period of rest and sight-seeing, the crew set forth to sail the *New Orleans* back upstream to Pittsburgh. They reached Natchez, and no farther. The steam plant, which had done so well downstream, became the little engine that couldn't. It strained and struggled but was unable to move the craft any farther against the current, so the dream of a round trip had to be abandoned. For the remaining two years of her brief existence, until she ran aground and sank, the *New Orleans* carried cotton and passengers on the Natchez-New Orleans run. She was a staunch pioneer—only a fragile forerunner of the luxurious packet boats that came later, true, but none of them faced as many adversities as she encountered.

Someone needed to invent a steamboat better than the *New Orleans*, one strong enough to go upstream as well as down. As so often had been the case in history, when an obvious problem existed, someone solved it. His name was Captain Henry Shreve.

River-wise from his years of running flatboats and keelboats, Shreve inspected the *New Orleans* and shook his head. He knew what was wrong with her. Fulton had designed her too much like an ocean-going ship; Shreve wanted a steamboat that was almost flat-bottomed and easily maneuvered. At a shipyard in Wheeling, West Virginia, in 1816, he built the boat that became the basic model for every river steamboat constructed after that. Patriotically, he called her the *Washington*.

First, Shreve built a hull that extended below the water's surface only two feet or so. Then he built a deck that extended not only the full width of the hull but far out over each side, an idea borrowed from the keelboats. Instead of installing the engine in the hold below deck level, as Fulton had done, Shreve put his engines right on the main deck and mounted them in a horizontal position, rather than vertical as Fulton had his. Fulton's boat had one engine, Shreve installed two, one attached to each side paddle wheel. This enabled the pilot to maneuver the vessel more easily; he could have one engine and paddle wheel running forward while the other engine was in reverse, helping him to turn the boat around rapidly. From the boilers of the two engines rose twin smokestacks. The boat sailed *on* the water, not *through* it.

Since the engines and boilers, and the stacks of wood to fire them,

The Washington *was designed to correct the* New Orleans' *faults. An artist's conception of the explosion that occurred in 1816.*

filled much of the main deck, Shreve built another deck on top for passenger cabins. Thus the *Washington* became the first double-decker and started the high-rise style in steamboats that led to additional decks later. Oddly, although the engines and boilers were situated on the main deck, the second deck was called "the boiler deck." On top he placed a glass-enclosed pilothouse.

"It looks like a floating dishpan," onlookers said when they saw the *Washington* with its wide overhanging lower deck close to the water.

The *Washington* demonstrated the value of Shreve's revolutionary ideas, despite a tragic accident. The vessel went up to Pittsburgh, took aboard a load of passengers and cargo, and headed for New Orleans. All went smoothly until she ran aground. As the crew struggled to free her, using all the power her engines could produce, a boiler blew up, spraying passengers and crew with scalding steam. Shreve and several others were blown overboard to safety. Burial services were held on the bank of the Ohio for those killed in the explosion, and the *Washington*, after lengthy repairs, sailed to New Orleans. After that, her luck was much better. She made a record run upstream. The next year she made a round trip between Louisville and New Orleans in only forty-one days, an unheard-of speed.

Everyone along the rivers realized that the age of the steamboat had arrived. Not only did Shreve conceive an efficient design, but he broke the monopoly Livingston and Fulton had obtained on steamboat travel in Louisiana by defying it. A United States Supreme Court decision wiped out their monopoly in New York, too. The right to sail the rivers was legally open to anyone who had a steamboat. The inland waters were free to all.

Soon Shreve produced another invention that made river travel safer and faster, an ungainly vessel called a snag boat. Snags were trees in the river, either floating mostly submerged or stuck to the

The steamboat Belle Zane *hits a partially submerged tree in the Mississippi River and sinks, with the loss of forty lives. The boat capsized during a frigid January night and sleeping passengers were thrown into the water without warning.*

bottom. If a steamboat ran into a snag, its wooden bottom could be ripped by the branches, and it could sink. The term "hitting a snag" that we use so much about any obstacle to our plans derives from these river obstructions. So many snags existed that steamboat men had names for different varieties. A *planter* was a tree trunk firmly wedged into the river bottom, but floating free at the top. A *sawyer* was a snag that bobbed up and down in the water. A log floating just below the surface was a *sleeper*. Call them by any name you wish, these lurking trees destroyed hundreds of flatboats, keelboats, and steamboats. So when Captain Shreve built a vessel with a jaw-like bow that pulled up snags and a sawmill on deck that cut them into short, harmless pieces, rivermen cheered. Shreveport, Louisiana, was named for the captain to honor him for clearing a mass of snags a hundred miles long that blocked navigation in the Red River.

Before long, in the 1820s, dozens of steamboats appeared along the big rivers. Some pushed up the Mississippi to the Minneapolis area and opened service on the upper river. Isolated communities began to feel as though they were in touch with the world, after all, because the steamboats brought them passengers and freight from "outside." Samuel Clemens, whom the world knows better as Mark Twain, told in his book *Life on the Mississippi* what his drowsy hometown of Hannibal, Missouri, was like when a steamboat arrived on a hot summer day during his boyhood.

The view from Hannibal up and down the Mississippi, he said, was restricted by points of land where the river curved.

"Precisely a film of dark smoke appears above one of the remote 'points'; instantly a Negro drayman, famous for his quick eye and prodigious voice, lifts up the cry, 'S-t-e-a-m-boat a-comin'!' and the scene changes! The town drunkard sits up, the clerks wake up, a furious clatter of drays follows, every house and store pours out a human contribution, and all in a twinkling the dead town is alive and moving. Drays, carts, men, boys, all go hurrying from their many quarters to a common center, the wharf. Assembled there, the people fasten their eyes upon the coming boat as upon a wonder they are seeing for the first time."

A bustle of unloading and loading follows, until the boat's bell rings and it departs.

Clemens adds, "After ten more minutes the town is dead again, and the town drunkard asleep by the skids once more."

And Tom Sawyer, the fictional Hannibal boy Clemens created from his own youthful memories, goes back to the chore of white-washing the picket fence outside his Aunt Polly's home, a few blocks from the river.

Those steamboats of the early period seemed wonderful to many, and, going downstream as fast as fifteen miles an hour, provided speed thrills no one had experienced before. To most people accustomed to traveling on foot or horseback, or floating on flatboats or keelboats, the steamboats were marvels of a new age. Some travelers more experienced in worldly luxuries had a different opinion, however. While admiring their speed, they found the boats noisy, dirty, and crowded. These travelers complained about swarms of mosquitoes and other unpleasant insects. Boat owners often were more interested in seeing how much cargo they could stack on the lower deck than they were in providing clean, spacious accommodations for passengers. These were to come in later decades when the ornate packet boats usually depicted in movies and in romantic books were put into service.

One such unhappy traveler was the renowned naturalist and creator of bird pictures, John James Audubon. He described the boat on which he traveled from Louisville to St. Louis as "the very filthiest of all filthy old rat-traps I ever traveled in; and the fare worse, certainly, much worse, and scanty withal that our worthy commander could not have given us another meal had we been detained a night longer." Audubon grumbled that the bed sheets were too small, the pillows were filled with bumpy cornhusks, the places for the passengers to wash were inadequate, and what's more, the roof of his cabin leaked.

That is how it was for a passenger traveling in "first-class" style. For most travelers, who went as cheap-fare deck passengers without cabins, conditions were worse. They were crushed together on the main deck, shoved against piles of cargo and firewood, and forced to breathe the hot, oily exhaust smells of the engines.

The famous English writer Charles Dickens rode on several steamboats during his American tour in 1842, and he complained especially about the crowded sleeping conditions. On a night boat down the Potomac River from Washington, he opened the door into the men's cabin and found this:

"To my horror and amazement it is full of sleepers in every stage, attitude, and variety of slumber: in the berths, on the chairs, on the floors, on the tables, and particularly around the stove . . . I count those slumbering passengers, and get past forty. There is no use in going further, so I begin to undress. As the chairs are all occupied, and there is nothing else to put my clothes on, I put them on the ground. . . . Having but partially undressed, I clamber on my shelf . . ."

On another steamboat, going down the Ohio from Pittsburgh to Cincinnati, Dickens was alarmed by the fire danger caused by the open doors of the unprotected boilers on the main deck. He calls it "a great body of fire that rages and roars beneath the frail pile of painted wood: the machinery, not warded off or guarded in any way, but doing its work in the midst of the crowd of idlers and emigrants and children, who throng the lower deck. . . ."

While Dickens disapproved of steamboats, he disliked boats on the canals even more. In his *American Notes* he had a few good things and many damning ones to say about travel on the man-made waterways which, like the navigable rivers, played such a vital part in the surge of migration westward.

CHAPTER THREE

Governor Clinton's Ditch

SINCE ancient days men have tried to improve on nature by digging waterways at places where they wished that a navigable river flowed, but none did. The Babylonians, the Egyptians, and the Chinese had canals more than two thousand years ago.

Visions of floating easily along canals, instead of struggling through swamps and forests, fascinated American settlers as they pushed inland from the Atlantic Coast. Even in colonial days proposals were made for canals. These became more frequent and more daring after the Revolutionary War, when families anxious to start a new life in the wilderness endured enormous hardships along the "traces," as the land trails were called.

Those settlers who crossed the mountains to the Ohio River could use the inland river system, as we have seen. But, while far less formidable than the Rocky Mountains that would challenge a later generation of migrants, the Appalachians formed a barrier that was not easily overcome. Going overland from New England and New York City to what we now call the Middle West and the western Great Lakes was so difficult that only a few rugged adventurers did so.

When we look at a map showing the mountain ranges of the eastern United States, it is apparent that one almost level path extends through the mountains—across New York State from the

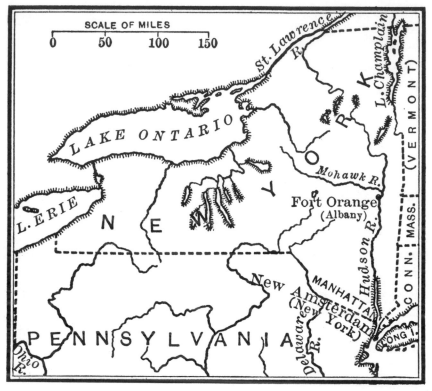

Old map of New York shows the almost level pass through the Appalachians formed by the Mohawk River and the Finger Lakes.

Hudson River at Albany to Lake Erie, just above Niagara Falls. The Hudson is at sea level. Some 350 miles to the west, Lake Erie at Buffalo is 555 feet higher than the Hudson River, not much of a rise over such a long distance. From Buffalo, travel by boat is easy west and north through the Great Lakes all the way to Minnesota.

While the route across New York looks attractive on the map, in the early 1800s the ground itself was a miserable morass of forest, swamps, and underbrush. As we drive across the state on the New York State Thruway past luxuriant green farmland, it is almost impossible to comprehend how forbidding the region looked then. Travelers in those days could go with some difficulty along the east-west Mohawk River valley through the eastern third of the state, but no similar river route was available in the western two-thirds.

Far-seeing men began to say, "If we built a canal across the state to Lake Erie, people and their goods could travel west on it. The boats could carry farm products back to Albany, and then down the Hudson to New York City."

"Impossible!" others replied. "It's much too far. We don't have the money. Our country doesn't have hydraulic engineers who know how to build a long canal."

Even President Thomas Jefferson, usually a man of remarkable vision, thought the idea of the Erie Canal was a ridiculous dream. When a delegation from New York called on him in Washington to seek federal money for constructing the canal, he turned them down resoundingly.

"It is a splendid project and may be executed a century hence," Jefferson told them.

"Why, sires, right near here is a canal of a few miles, projected by General Washington, which, if completed, would render this a fine commercial city, which has languished many years because the small sum of $200,000 necessary to complete it, cannot be obtained from the general government or from individuals.

"And you talk of making a canal three hundred and fifty miles long through a wilderness! It is little short of madness to think of it at this day."

A very determined man was certain that President Jefferson was wrong. He was DeWitt Clinton, who led the long fight for the canal and then directed its construction. As mayor of New York, Clinton realized that such a canal would make his city an important port for immigrants and commodities from Europe. He didn't like to see Philadelphia and Boston ahead of New York in importance. As United States Senator and later governor of New York, he

DeWitt Clinton, who made the dream of the Erie Canal come true

battled relentlessly for the canal plan and to raise money for construction. Finally, the state legislature agreed to pay the costs. What a bargain it got!

Engineers went to England and Europe to learn how to build locks and do the water engineering that was necessary to keep the canal channel full.

The plan the engineers and politicians finally agreed upon was for a canal 363 miles long, starting east from the tiny settlement at Buffalo to Rochester; continuing through the treacherous Montezuma Swamp to Syracuse; south of Lake Oneida to Rome; alongside the Mohawk River to Utica, Little Falls, and Schenectady; then entering the Hudson River at Albany. The "big ditch" was to be forty feet wide at ground level and twenty-eight feet wide at the bottom, and four feet deep.

When construction crews began work on July 4, 1817, digging east and west from Rome, they faced formidable obstacles.

Even with modern bulldozers and other motorized earth-moving equipment, digging such a long trench would be difficult. On the Erie Canal, the only tools men had at the start were shovels and wheelbarrows. First they marked the right-of-way by driving lines of stakes sixty feet apart, to show the outer boundaries of the route to be cleared. Inside these, two more lines of stakes were placed forty feet apart, to indicate the edges of the waterway itself. Mile after mile, these lines of stakes stretched through woods and under-brush that, never before disturbed by man, had grown into an intertwined thicket of branches above ground and a jumble of roots underground.

Soon the workmen devised crude but effective tools to speed up the land clearing and digging. They brought in horses to pull plows that broke the crust of the ground. Behind the plows came scrapers, also pulled by horses, that dragged the loosened dirt up the sides of the ditch. This dirt was used to build a towpath ten feet wide along one bank; here the teams of horses or mules that pulled the canalboats would walk. Always there was work to be done by gangs of men jabbing shovels into the dirt. Somebody realized that by attaching long, sharp blades to the sides of the plow, he could cut underbrush at the same time the plow blade broke the ground. The idea went into general use.

Trees in the canal's path were pulled down by chains tied to

1817
Section of Original Erie in cut greater than 9ft. according to specifications.

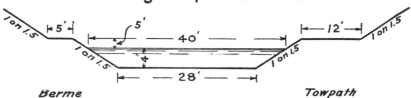

Berme   Towpath

*Diagram of the Erie Canal. "Berme" re-
fers to the bank opposite the towpath.*

their tops. Stumps, with their long tenacles of roots, presented an especially difficult problem. Since dynamite had not yet been invented to blast them out, the men had to remove them by tedious digging. An ingenious workman invented a stump-puller that looked strange but worked. Two wooden wheels sixteen feet in diameter were connected by a huge axle thirty feet long. Midway in the axle there was a drumlike wheel fourteen feet in diameter. A chain was attached from a stump to this middle wheel, and a rope that was wrapped around the wheel was tied to a pair of horses on the other side. Urged on by the cracking of whips, the straining horses put their full strength into their harness and dragged the stump from the ground.

Seven men with two horses could pull forty stumps in a fourteen-hour day. Compared to the progress before the stump-puller was invented, that seemed wonderful to the Erie workmen; when compared to the vastness of the forest through which the canal was charted, it gives some idea of the immensity of their task.

Mostly, the canal was dug by Irishmen. Immigrants from Ireland arrived in New York City by the thousands, needing jobs in their new country, at the same time the Erie Canal builders desperately sought laborers. Representatives of canal contractors met the im-

Workers of a later date put finishing touches on a canal lock.

The Chief Engineer of Rome, *first
boat to pass through the Erie Canal*

migrant ships as they docked, signed up the husky Irishmen, put
them on sailing sloops up the Hudson River to Albany, and had
them swinging shovels in the Erie trench within a few days.

At one point, three thousand Irishmen were at work on the
canal. They slugged away at the back-breaking job for low pay.
Rations of whiskey were doled out to them several times a day.
When the canal was being pushed through the dank, dreary Montezuma Swamp, the Irishmen worked in water and muck above their
waists. Ferocious swarms of mosquitoes swirling around their heads
drove them frantic. More than the discomfort, the mosquitoes
brought malaria, causing more than a thousand of the workers to
become ill. Many died: no records were kept, so nobody knows
how many.

The Erie Canal was not built straight through from one end to
the other. Sections were assigned to different contractors, who
worked at varying speeds. As the first years of construction passed,
the canal route took on a patchwork look—a few miles completed
here and there, while adjacent sections had hardly been touched.
Canalboats began operating on sections as they were finished,
giving travelers a tantalizing taste of what awaited them when and
if the big ditch finally was completed.

Not everybody thought it would be. Governor Clinton's political
opponents did their best to block the work by holding back money
for construction. Lacking Clinton's vision of what the canal would
do to open the West, these short-sighted men were primarily interested in defeating him politically. For awhile he left the governorship and was forced off the Canal Commission, which supervised construction. This act of petty jealousy made the public so
angry that he soon returned to both the governorship and the

View of the aqueduct at Rexford, where the canal carried canalboats over the Mohawk River.

commission. Thus, even while the canal was being built, its future hung in doubt.

Perhaps it isn't surprising that many people became impatient and dubious, because the canal took so long to build. Eight years passed from the day ground was broken in 1817 until the Erie was finished in 1825. Work halted during the winter snow and in periods of heavy rain when the canal became a quagmire. It was, after all, only a very long hole in the raw earth and it filled quickly with mud and ooze.

Clinton and the canal builders saved the hardest parts of the job, at opposite ends of the route, until the last.

At the eastern end, the canal's course from its junction with the Hudson River was up a narrow, sharply sloping stretch of the Mohawk River that boiled with waterfalls and rapids. The canal was to run alongside the river in that area. From Albany to Schenectady, fifteen miles northwest, the canal had to be carried across the Mohawk River twice over long aqueducts, one of which stretched 1188 feet. Within that short, precipitous distance, the engineers had to build twenty-seven locks that would raise or lower the boats to new water levels.

The principal of the canal lock is simple. The water in a canal must be level at all times; no current should flow through the channel. In sloping areas where water runs downgrade, locks are necessary so the boats can be taken down bit by bit, like walking downstairs. A lock resembles an open-topped stone box placed in a canal, with gates that swing open at each end. When a boat comes downstream, it floats into the boxlike lock chamber. The downstream gate is closed when it enters. The gate at the upstream end then is shut behind the boat; the water in the lock is drained out, lowering the boat; the downstream gate is opened and the boat is pulled out at the lower water level. The process is reversed when the boat is going upstream.

Altogether, eighty-three locks were built along the 363 miles of Erie Canal. They were made with blocks of stone held together by

A canalboat "locking through" Lock 22, Rexford, New York, 1909

a special kind of lime rock deposit called hydraulic cement, which by good luck was found near the canal route. The surviving portions of these locks, still to be seen at a few places across New York, show the craftsmanship of the Erie's builders, especially when we remember that they knew little about the job when they began and had to learn by trial and error.

The same is true of the aqueducts. Perhaps the most dramatic of these structures was over the Genesee River at Rochester. It was 804 feet long, the longest stone-arch bridge in North America, and was supported by eleven Roman arches, on top of which was a superstructure that carried the canal aloft like an airborne river. Splendid looking as it was, this aqueduct had a flaw—it leaked. In winter, water dripping from it formed gigantic icicles. After twenty years it was replaced by a longer, wider, waterproof aqueduct that still stands 140 years later. Being pulled across the Genesee Aqueduct in a canalboat and looking far down into the river valley was an exciting moment for travelers.

Of all the locks in the Erie, those at Lockport near the western end of the ditch were the most difficult to build. They had to be hewn from the rock of the Niagara Escarpment, a massive upthrust that rises above the level ground. It is from this same ridge that Niagara Falls was carved seventeen miles to the west by the flow of the Niagara River.

The challenge was to lower eastbound boats seventy feet from the rocky ledge to the plain. Elsewhere the canal had single locks, through which boats going in opposite directions took turns passing. At Lockport, double locks were built to permit boats to pass through in both directions simultaneously. Five sets of locks were constructed up the cliff; these became known to canalers as the Lockport Five.

Because they had neither dynamite nor nitroglycerin, the Irish laborers had to blast out the lock chambers with black powder or blasting powder. Dangerous stuff it was, too. If it wasn't handled carefully, it could blow off a man's fingers or an arm, or kill him. Quite a few men were maimed and some died because they were

46

Set of five locks known as the Lockport Five carried canalboats up and down the Niagara Escarpment.

too impatient, or too curious. After a hole was drilled in the rock, powder was stuffed into it, and a fuse or trail of powder was laid out for some distance. A workman ignited the fuse and ran for shelter. If things worked properly, the flame sped up the fuse and ignited the charge. Sometimes the anticipated period before the explosion passed but no big bang occurred. So a workman went up to see why the fuse had stopped burning, only to have the rocks explode in his face.

Life became perilous for residents of the little village of Lockport during the weeks of blasting. They were in the line of fire.

One of them, "Aunt Edna" Smith, told in her memoirs how rocks several inches in diameter rained down on the town. Whenever they heard the warning shout, "Look out!" the residents ran for cover. They built lean-tos of tree trunks placed closely together along the sides of their houses, under which they took shelter from flying rocks. At night the Irishmen slept in the lean-tos.

One young lawyer of Lockport, who later became a judge, was relaxing in his office one day with his chair tilted back and his feet on the edge of a table. *Bang*! went a blast. A heavy rock was blown through the front door, rolled across the floor, and knocked the chair from under him. *Thud*! went the attorney.

When the Marquis de Lafayette, the Frenchman who had helped the American cause so much during the Revolutionary War, made his nostalgic tour of the young United States in 1825, the Erie Canal was open from Lockport eastward. Only the portion over the Niagara Escarpment remained unfinished, and the men worked with every ounce of muscle they had to finish it in time for a grand opening later that year. Construction bosses urged them on by placing barrels of whiskey at points along the route ahead, like a carrot on a stick, as prizes waiting to be claimed when the work reached each barrel.

Word came that Lafayette would arrive at Buffalo by steamboat on Lake Erie, then travel by road to Lockport and board a canalboat there. Here was an opportunity for the canal workmen to show their stuff. As the elegant French nobleman in powdered wig was escorted out of the forest into Lockport by a welcoming committee on horseback, a thunderous blast greeted him. The uproar resembled the firing of dozens of cannon in quick succession, a regular artillery barrage. Even the rock-splattered residents of Lockport had never heard such a commotion. The workmen had their special way of saying, "Vive Lafayette!" They had placed

Lockport in the 1830's. It must have looked much like this when Lafayette made his historic visit.

charges of powder at close intervals along the rocky edge of the locks and connected them by trails of black powder. Someone touched them off when Lafayette came into view. When the noise quieted, he told the welcoming committee that he was "much pleased" by the greeting—and probably more than a little astonished. 'Twas a great day for the French there in the wilderness, provided by the Irish.

At last, in October, 1825, the Erie Canal was finished. Governor Clinton, the builders, and indeed the entire United States had reason for triumphant celebration. The water highway through the wilderness was finally in operation and already throngs of settlers and heavy tonnage of freight moved along it. More than any other single route, the Erie Canal opened the door to the American heartland.

As was suitable, the celebration was in a grand style. It lasted nine days, climaxing in a ceremony known as the Wedding of the Waters.

Clinton's "Big Ditch" opened the way to waves of immigrants.

The packet boat *Seneca Chief* left Buffalo eastbound on October 26, 1825, carrying Governor Clinton. Four other packets made up the official party, and many other boatmen added their craft to the procession as it moved slowly across New York. The official party's boats were painted in brilliant colors, and on the deck of the *Seneca Chief* stood two large oil paintings, one of the canal and the other of Clinton dressed as Hercules. Also on the *Seneca*'s deck were two kegs painted in patriotic colors. One held water from Lake Erie, the other from famous rivers around the world.

Since no telegraph, telephone, radio, or television existed then, there was no obvious way to flash ahead word that Clinton's boat was on its way and the canal was officially open. That didn't stop the happy celebrants. Cannon had been placed at intervals along the entire length of the canal and down the Hudson River from Albany to New York City, close enough together that each gun's crew could hear the sound of its neighbor.

At ten o'clock that morning, the cannon at the Buffalo harbor was fired. Then the next one to the east, and the next, sending the news in a ripple of sound mile after mile. The cannonaded message traveled more than five hundred miles from Buffalo to New York City in eighty minutes, touching off cheering along the route. The New York City gun fired a return greeting, which bounced back to Buffalo in the same length of time.

Clinton's triumphal procession was much slower. At almost every town along the Erie, many of which hadn't existed before construction began, he was greeted with speeches. Banquet after banquet hailed the party. At night, arches bearing messages of congratulation that spanned the canal were illuminated by whale-oil lamps.

More significant than many of the long-winded speeches was the fact that at one point Governor Clinton passed a westbound boat carrying the first party of immigrants to come to the United States from Norway. These men, women, and children had traveled for more than three months across the Atlantic Ocean on a sailing vessel and now were riding along the canal to a wilderness area in upper New York to start farms. Eventually, many of them moved on farther west to the Great Plains. They were typical of the immigrant throng, up to forty thousand a year at times, that followed the Erie Canal to populate the West.

Clinton deserved all the gratitude he received, but he must have grown a little weary of the oratory and food and cheering by the time the *Seneca Chief* was towed down the Hudson by a steamboat into New York City.

Early on the morning of November 4, as shore guns boomed, the *Seneca Chief* was pulled down New York Harbor to Sandy Hook. While hundreds of boat whistles pierced the air, Clinton ceremoniously poured the keg of Lake Erie water into the Atlantic, to symbolize the ocean's link with the Great Lakes. Then he dumped the contents of the second keg overboard, this time to symbolize that cargo from faraway areas of the world was able to move by water far into the central part of the United States.

What a gala day it was!

CHAPTER FOUR

A Ride on the Young Lion

LET'S take a trip on America's finest limited-access highway of 150 years ago. The route is long, more than 350 miles, smooth, and level because its surface is water. All crossroads pass over it on bridges. There are no traffic lights. The speed limit is enforced strictly—four miles an hour!

Our vehicle for this journey west on the Erie Canal is a wooden packet boat bravely named *Young Lion of the West*. She is eighty feet long and flat bottomed, painted gaily in red and yellow with her name in ornate gold scrollwork letters on the stern. She is narrow, only eleven feet wide, and barely eight feet high. A flat-roofed cabin extends most of her length, with a narrow catwalk around its base. Red and white calico curtains cover the windows. On the cabin roof, women in hoop skirts and men, many of whom wear tall top hats, sit on benches and watch the scenery slide past.

The *Young Lion of the West* is propelled along the Big Ditch by mulepower, three "long-eared robins" harnessed in tandem pulling the boat at the end of a long towrope. At the stern, a steersman handles a tiller bar whose rudder holds the boat straight in the channel.

We go aboard the *Young Lion* at Schenectady. Like many other passengers, we traveled from Albany on the Hudson River by stagecoach, to avoid the tedious trip through the twenty-seven locks that a boat must navigate between the two cities.

Steersman's horn announces arrival of Erie Canal packet at a town.

The steersman sounds a deep blast on the boat's horn. A bell rings. "We're leaving!" someone calls, and two laggard passengers who have been talking on the wharf jump aboard at the last moment. Even if they hadn't made the jump, they could have caught up with the boat by jogging along the towpath to the first bridge on the route and dropping from it onto the deck when the *Young Lion* reached them. Passengers often make side excursions ashore on foot as the boat moves along and rejoin it at the next bridge or lock.

Stepping into the cabin, we find a long rectangular room with ceiling so low that tall passengers must bend over to keep from bumping their heads. Tables have been joined together in a single row almost the length of the cabin, with dishes and cutlery laid for supper. At the front is a red curtain, and beyond that the ladies' cabin.

"If this is the dining cabin, where will we sleep?" is the question that immediately comes to mind. More than seventy men, women, and children are aboard, and no bunks are to be seen.

"You will find out soon enough," a veteran traveler tells us.

Through the cabin windows there isn't much to see because the canal banks obscure the view. That must be why most of the passengers are up on the cabin roof deck. No sooner have we joined

The towpath through Schenectady

them up above than a shouted warning comes from the bow. "Bridge!" The steersman calls out, "Low bridge!" Everyone stoops as the bottom of the bridge passes inches over our heads. Passengers who don't heed that warning may suffer severe injuries to their heads or find themselves knocked overboard into the muddy water of the canal.

There is that cry again, "Bridge!" And again, and again. Since hundreds of bridges cross the canal, so the farmers can drive their livestock and wagons from one side to the other, in some sections the passengers are almost constantly bobbing up and down. The canal builders constructed the bridges as low as possible, to save money on building materials.

As our boat glides along the canal, sometimes through forest so close that we can almost touch the branches, sometimes past farm fields, the scene is peaceful. Gentle sounds of water slapping against the boat's hull and the hoofs of the mules *clop-clop*ping on the hard dirt towpath mingle with the sounds of birds and, far too often,

An early drawing of the Erie Canal

the angry buzz of mosquitoes. Our mules could pull the boat faster than four miles an hour, at least for short stretches, but that maximum speed has been set by the Erie's managers because when boats go faster they slosh waves against the dirt banks of the canal and cause dangerous erosion. Even though we wish we could go faster, a smooth ride at four miles an hour is far better than bouncing and jostling in a wagon along a rutted dirt track at a slower pace.

After we have traveled for about three hours, the captain orders the boat to tie up against the bank near a building. This proves to be a stable. Our team of mules is unhitched and a fresh team put in

A change of mules along the towpath

place at the end of the towrope. When the boat starts up again, the pace is a little faster, as the fresh mules trot ahead briskly under the crack of our driver's bullwhip.

When suppertime comes, we go down into the cabin and find seats at the long table. Food is brought from the cook's galley at the rear. What a mixture it is: bread and butter, salmon, shad, liver, steak, potatoes, pickles, ham, chops, sausages, and puddings. Nobody goes hungry.

When we go back up on the deck in the twilight, our *Young Lion of the West* overtakes another canalboat, also headed west. As a luxury packet boat that carries only passengers, no freight, we have the right of way under canal rules over the slower "line boats" that transport freight as well as people. Line boats in turn outrank the ponderous freight boats that creep along at barely a mile an hour.

But how does our boat pass the one ahead? Both are moving along the right side of the canal, with towropes trailing taut about seventy-five yards back from the mule teams on the towpath to the boats' bows. Soon we find out.

Our captain blows his horn as a signal to the captain ahead. Then comes a tricky maneuver. The boat in front stops, close to the right-hand bank. Our steersman turns the *Young Lion* out into the middle of the canal. At the same time, our team of mules gets off to the far right edge of the towpath. As the *Young Lion* drifts abreast of the line boat, the latter's crewmen lift our towropes over their boat and their team of mules and pass the line forward until it drops into the water ahead of their bow. Our team of mules resumes its trot, and we pull ahead.

As we pass close by, we see the other boat crowded with people, many in odd-looking clothing, immigrants from Europe headed for a new home. The deck is jammed with furniture and trunks, a woman is cooking supper on an open stove at the stern, and crates of squawking chickens add a rural touch. When we try to talk to the immigrants, they wave and call back in a language we can't understand.

A barefoot canalboatman at the tiller

Here comes a packet toward us, with a whale-oil lamp on its front flickering in the dusk. Since there is a towpath only on our side of the canal, the other boat's mules are coming straight toward ours. How can we pass without getting our towropes tangled?

Again the canal rules solve the problem. Since the other packet is moving east, which is called downstream because of that 550-foot drop in altitude between Lake Erie and the Hudson, it has the right of way. Its captain blows two blasts on his horn, orders his mules to the outer edge of the towpath, stops his boat by the downstream bank, and lets the towline fall limp into the water all the way to the bottom. Our captain then maneuvers our boat over the sunken tow-

It was pleasanter on top than inside a packet boat, at least in good weather.

line, keeping our mules close to the water edge of the towpath. When we have passed safely over the towline and beyond the other boat's team, the captains exchange toots of their horns and go ahead.

Dark has fallen, and it is time for bed. The women and small children retire into the curtained ladies' cabin. Now we will find out where and how we will sleep. The captain calls the male passengers into the dining-room cabin, and we find a sight quite different from what it was at suppertime. The long dining table has been cleared and divided into several small ones down the middle of the room. Along each side of the cabin narrow metal shelves three tiers high have been plugged into wall sockets to form the frames of berths, and ropes are suspended from the ceilings to hold them steady. Thin canvas is stretched over each frame.

The captain announces, "We will draw the numbers of your berths by lot. After you have your berth, please retire immediately."

"But there are more men passengers than there are berths," a man exclaimed.

"Those who don't get numbers for berths must sleep on the floor or on the tables."

What happens after that has some funny moments. Some men undress, at least part way, and lay their clothing on any chairs they can find. Others don't bother, merely removing their shoes and wrapping themselves in cloaks on the thin mattresses that are given us to spread on our shelves.

Watching a fat man climb up to a top bunk, until his nose is just a few inches from the deck above when he lies down, makes other passengers laugh, especially when he turns on his side and falls off the narrow shelf to the floor. Most passengers take these mishaps in good humor. When you lie on a middle or lower berth and have a heavy man above you, his weight makes the canvas sag in a half circle until it almost hits your face.

And the snoring! Buzz-saw sounds, sudden loud snorts like explosions, high-pitched whines—they mingle in the dark into a weird blend of sounds so disturbing that many of the men, already aching from the narrow, hard bunks, can't sleep. The air is stifling. All night long, passengers get up, stumble into sleepers on the floor, and prowl out on deck for fresh air. Some want to sleep on deck but are told it is forbidden. Too dangerous, because of the bridges.

We hear snoring from the other side of the red curtain, too—ladylike sounds, but no more tuneful than from our side. And the cries of babies.

Nights are long on the canalboats.

Morning finally comes. Early, too, at 5:00 A.M. We must leave

Mornings were welcomed as a chance to get back on deck, even though there was not much to do except watch the peaceful scenery.

The sight of a town or settle-ment meant a chance for a little diversion with side trips to canal-side stores.

the cabin so it can be made over into a dining room for breakfast. Shivering in the cold dawn, we go forward to the wash-up area to wait our turns for a clean-up. Nobody takes very long at it. A thin ladle is chained to the deck. You dip that over the side into the brownish canal water and pour the contents into a tin basin, also chained to the deck to stop thieves. After you have washed in the basin, you may use the public towel, comb, and hairbrush fastened to the wall. How refreshing it feels after that long, uncomfortable night!

After that, the hot food at breakfast tastes wonderful.

Following breakfast, many of the passengers jump off the boat and walk alongside it on the towpath. Keeping up isn't difficult, and we know that if we fall behind, we can catch up at the lock a mile or so ahead. Some of us fall in step with the driver of the mule team pulling the towrope. He is only a boy, thin and in ragged clothes.

"How old are you?" someone asks.

"Twelve."

60

A three-horse tandem hitch, a hoggee or driver, and a canalboat

"Don't you go to school?"

"Naw. Never do."

Another man wonders how much he is paid and how many hours a day he walks the towpath or straddles one of the mules.

"Us hoggees get eight dollars a month. Except some captains try to cheat you out of it. Me and the other boy each drive twelve hours a day, six hours on and six off. In between, we sleep and eat on the boat—and polish harness."

"Don't you get time off to go home?"

"My paw's dead and my maw disappeared. I don't have a home. In winter when the canal's closed I sleep in a stable in Buffalo."

"Doesn't anybody care that you work like this?"

"Who'd care? I need the money."

As we approach the lock, everyone around the gates seems angry. Half a dozen boats are lined up at each end of the lock, waiting to get through. Horses and mules and drivers and passengers are milling around in a noisy, confused mess.

Instead of waiting his turn at the end of the westbound line, our captain blows his horn, steers the *Young Lion of the West* out into mid-channel, and demands that the crews on the waiting boats pass our towrope ahead over their boats. They do so, but curse us for cutting in ahead of them. Soon we are at the front of the line. That is the canal rule. Packets take priority over everyone at a lock, no matter how long the others have waited.

An eastbound boat has come out of the lock, and it is our turn. The *Young Lion* is pulled into the lock, the gates behind us are closed, and on deck we find ourselves surrounded by the high stone walls and wooden gates. Vents in the sides of the lock chamber are

Early lock gates were opened and closed by hand, using the horizontal wooden bars at the top. Pictured is the entrance lock into the Erie Canal at Troy.

opened, water rushes in, and soon we realize that the boat is rising. Within five minutes the water level inside the lock is the same as that in the canal beyond the upstream gate. The tenders pull the gate open, and our mules drag us along the canal at an elevation several feet higher than we were before the lock.

The first day the *Young Lion of the West* traveled nearly eighty miles. It is difficult to believe that people can go so far, so fast. Just three more days, and we will be in Buffalo!·

CHAPTER FIVE

A Case of Canal Fever

A PECULIAR disease called "canal fever" afflicted many of the raw pioneer states as far west as the Mississippi River after they saw the success of the Erie Canal. Symptoms seen in the leaders of these states included a glint in the eye for profits and itchy palms anxious to collect money from tolls.

The Erie Canal made a profit from the day it was opened and soon paid back the seven-million-dollar cost of building it. Envious, the legislatures of other states asked themselves, "Why don't we build canals, too?" During the twenty-five years that followed the Erie's opening in 1825, hundreds of miles of canals were built or attempted in states from Maryland on the Atlantic Coast to Illinois on the Mississippi River.

Few of the canals in these states made a profit; most of them lost money. Some never were completed. Others had insufficient water and ran dry in summer. The sparsely settled state of Indiana spent so much money on the Wabash and Erie Canal and other lesser projects, and took in such small tolls, that the state treasury went bankrupt.

Although none of these man-made waterways came close to the success of the Erie Canal, they had an extremely important role in the opening of the West. They made it possible for pioneer families to move into unsettled regions of states such as Ohio, Indiana, and Illinois, and to ship out their farm products. Like the Erie, they became routes along which news and cultural interests flowed. It is difficult for us to realize how isolated and lonely frontier towns often were. When a canal passed through a town, it became a link between the settlers and the outside world.

William Dean Howells, an important novelist and critic, grew up during the 1840s in a village along the Miami and Erie Canal in Ohio, which ran south more than two hundred miles from Lake Erie to the Ohio River. The purpose of it and a parallel canal farther east was to connect the Great Lakes and the Ohio-Mississippi River system. He tells about the excitement in his village when the daily canal packet arrived from Dayton.

"To my boy's young vision, this craft was of . . . incomparable lightness and grace," he wrote in his memoirs. "When she came in of a summer evening her deck was thronged with people, and the captain stood with his right foot on the spring catch that held the towrope. The water curled away on either side of her sharp prow, that cut its way onward at the full rate of five miles an hour, and the team came swinging down the towpath at a gallant trot, the driver sitting the hindmost horse of three, and cracking his long-lashed whip with loud explosions, as he whirled its snaky spirals in the air. All of the boys in town were there, meekly proud to be

A team of mules wearing special harness to keep off flies pulls a boat along the Miami and Erie Canal in Ohio, near Cincinnati.

Many of the crewmen's families lived on the Erie canalboats. The women washed clothing by hand and hung it out to dry on a clothesline strung along the cabin roof.

ordered out of his way, to break and fly before his volleyed oaths and far before his horses' feet; and suddenly the captain pressed his foot on the spring and released the towrope. The driver kept on to the stable with unslackened speed, and the line followed him, swishing and skating over the water, while the steersman put his helm hard aport, and the packet rounded to, and swam softly and slowly up to her moorings. No steamer arrives from Europe now with such thrilling majesty."

Since no laws against child labor existed then, boys became towpath drivers as soon as they could handle horses or mules. Driving a canalboat team seemed as glamorous to boys then as driving a locomotive did to their grandsons, until they actually went to work at the job. At one time, an estimated ten thousand boys worked on the canals in New York State, for about half the wages men were paid for doing the same jobs. It wasn't easy, either. The teams of horses or mules had to be urged on with whips, yet soothed and controlled when the boats and teams milled around the locks. If an animal fell into the canal, the boy had to jump in, capture it, and swim to a place on the bank where both could scramble ashore, all the while being cursed by his captain as a clumsy oaf.

Long before he became President, James A. Garfield worked as a driver on the Ohio and Erie Canal.

Often the canal boys were homeless orphans for whom nobody took responsibility. They were overworked, underpaid, and exposed to hardships and to the bullying of the brawling, drinking, roughneck men who loafed around the canal saloons. An eleven-year-old boy was expected to do a man's work; if he didn't he might be beaten by his master.

Worst off were immigrant boys from Europe without families, who were put up on the bidding block in New York Harbor by the captains of the ships on which they had crossed the Atlantic. The bidder who claimed each boy paid the captain the cost of the boy's ocean crossing, then had the right to the boy's work for a year or more without paying him anything.

One young canal driver who learned quickly to protect himself on the towpaths was named Jimmie Garfield. At the age of sixteen he was driving for the *Evening Star* on the Ohio and Erie Canal. Approaching Akron, his boat and a boat coming from a side canal raced to see which could reach the lock first. The other boat finished slightly ahead. A jeering boatman yelled obscene taunts at Jimmie. Garfield became so angry that he hurled his fifteen-foot bullwhip at the man and knocked him down. Jimmie then maneuvered his boat into the lock first. History knows Jimmie as James A. Garfield, President of the United States.

The young boatmen had their bits of fun, too, especially with the backwoodsmen who built their own amateurish boats and sailed them on the canals with skimpy knowledge of what they were doing. One such makeshift craft launched by a farmer and two of his farmhands reached a town on the Erie Canal on its first night afloat. The farmer-turned-sailor tied it up for the night at the boat basin. While he and the crew slept aboard, a group of youths unfastened the boat, turned it around, and tied it up again. The next morning, while the pranksters watched, the landlubber sailors departed down the canal—in the wrong direction. The scenery looked a bit familiar to them at times, but they kept going until they reached the next town.

"This is the same place we passed through yesterday, going the other way!" the amazed farmer exclaimed.

Turning around again, they had to endure the horselaughs of the canalside hangers-on when they brought their boat back to its morning starting point.

For the passengers on canalboats, boredom was a problem. Hour after hour of watching scenery crawl past became monotonous,

View of two locks, the Rexford Aqueduct carrying the Erie Canal across the Mohawk River (extreme left background), and a feeder or side canal in the left foreground.

but few forms of entertainment were to be found on the boats. Sometimes passengers staged races with cockroaches, grasshoppers, or frogs. It was easy to find such creatures on or around the boat. A circle was drawn on the deck and the "coaches" of the cockroach racers held them in the middle of the ring. Bets were placed, the coach of each insect released it, and the first cockroach to crawl outside the circle was the winner. Loud cheers for the winner echoed in the surrounding forest.

While most of the boats carried passengers and/or freight, others moved slowly along the waterways providing supplies and amusement for the canalers and townspeople. Floating stores and saloons sold their wares to passing boats that tied up briefly alongside. Fast-talking hucksters on medicine showboats peddled patent medicines, mostly useless, to bankside audiences, then moved on. Occasionally a showboat, or a group of them tied together to form a stage, entertained the people of a town with a melodrama or minstrel show, illuminated by flares or whale-oil lamps. Poor as these shows usually were, they brightened the often dull existence in the remote towns.

Busy as it was, the Erie Canal operated only for about eight months each year because the stern upper New York State winters shut it down. When the winter freeze and snowstorms set in, all traffic stopped. The canal was drained; otherwise it would have become a 350-mile-long cake of ice. Boats, as a rule, rested on the mud bottom of the empty canal until spring, while crew members hunted temporary jobs, loafed, or went back to the farm. Boating families often lived aboard their craft grounded in the ooze, while their boys and girls went to school in the nearest town. Work crews cleaned up the canal bottom, removing the soggy mass of debris that had accumulated, either having been dropped overboard or blown into the water by the wind. In the spring, repair gangs patched holes in the canal banks that had been caused by gnawing muskrats or by erosion. Then water was turned in again, and a new canal season began.

Pennsylvania sought to catch up with her rival New York's Erie Canal by building a system of waterways from Philadelphia on the Atlantic Coast across the state to Pittsburgh. From there, travelers

Confederate Army soldiers aboard a transport barge on the James River Canal in Virginia being moved to a battle area during the Civil War. The team is far ahead on the towpath.

could continue their trips west aboard steamboats down the Ohio River. But the Alleghany Mountains formed a high, solid, north-south barricade across the path of the canal. Even with the aid of dozens of locks, canal water could not be lifted over the mountain barrier. But the canalboats went over the mountains, nevertheless—aboard railroad cars!

This was accomplished by the famous Alleghany Portage Railroad at Hollidaysburg, running a distance of thirty-seven miles—ten miles up the eastern slope of the mountains and twenty-six miles down the western side. Each slope had a series of five inclines, with fairly level stretches in between. The crest of the mountain was 1398 feet high.

A westbound boat was towed by animals to the end of the canal at the foot of the mountain. The canalboat was floated forward until it came to rest on top of a railroad flatcar standing on a submerged track. A stationary engine pulled the flatcar along the rails out of the water and up the incline. Then horses dragged the boat-laden flatcar from the top of the first incline to the foot of the next one. There another stationary engine took hold; another team of horses was hooked on at the top of the second incline; and so on until flatcar and boat reached the mountain crest. After the boat's passengers stayed overnight at a trackside inn, they rode in railroad carriages down the inclined levels on the western slope until they reached another section of the canal. There the boat was refloated and pulled to Pittsburgh by a team of horses or mules. Some of the longer canalboats could be divided into two parts, front and back, thus splitting the load for the portage onto two flatcars. Each boat was put together again in the canal at the bottom of the western slope. What a laborious way to travel that was! Still, it was faster than using the mountain trails, and more comfortable, too.

Despite the difficulties involved, thousands and thousands of settlers moved west along this route. Although the Pennsylvania Grand Canal never rivaled the Erie Canal in the number of travelers carried, its role in the westward migration was significant.

When Charles Dickens made the Pennsylvania canal trip, he was impressed, if not a little startled, by the mountain heights his party scaled on the portage. He wrote, "Occasionally the rails are laid upon the extreme verge of a giddy precipice; and looking from the carriage window, the traveler gazes sheer down, without a stone or scrap of fence between, into the mountain depths below."

No other canal trip could offer quite *that* kind of a ride.

Among the other best-known canals during the period of "canal fever" were the Delaware and Hudson, the Chesapeake and Ohio, the Illinois-Michigan, and the Blackstone in Massachusetts and Rhode Island.

During the 1850s, just before the Civil War, railroad engines began to point their sharp-nosed cowcatchers along newly laid tracks west of the Alleghany Mountains. When they did, the canal boom died. Who wanted to loaf on a canal at four miles an hour when a passenger train rolled along at fifteen or twenty miles an hour? The canal trip from Philadelphia to Pittsburgh required six days. When the Pennsylvania Railroad was built along a parallel route, its trains made the same trip in fifteen hours. Trains were more comfortable, too, and could go wherever tracks were laid, not just along a canal path. Naturally, travelers switched to the trains, removing one of the primary reasons the canals existed. The other was freight. Again, trains were much faster than the freightboats and got the farmers' crops to market sooner. Some of the canals in Ohio and Indiana lost almost all their business to railroads just a few years after they were opened, leaving the state governments with heavy debts for their construction.

Not the amazing Erie Canal, however. A railroad built across New York State on the "water level route" paralleling the canal did draw away the canal's passengers. That actually pleased the canal managers, because freight traffic on the Erie had become so heavy that the passenger boats had come to be considered a nuisance by shippers. The Erie Canal was widened and deepened, and then enlarged again. Finally it was rebuilt as the New York State Barge Canal, which now as a deep, wide channel carries hundreds of large barges, propelled by diesel engines, loaded with oil and other bulk cargoes from the Hudson River into Lake Erie. It is DeWitt Clinton's dream come true, blown up a hundred times beyond its original scope.

While the New York canal and other freight channels flourish today, the only passengers to ride on them are occasional guests of the barge company managements and a few tourists in modern packets. Instead, travelers in automobiles whiz alongside—or cross over—weed-grown remnants of the old canals here and there. They talk about how romantic it must have been to ride a canalboat—and then they spend the night on soft king-sized mattresses in air-conditioned motel rooms.

Canal fever in the United States lasted only about thirty years. Steamboats were plying the rivers when it began and were still puffing and snorting ahead long after it had died out. Steamboats and canalboats never were rivals but were more like partners in the enormous task of moving Americans around their expanding country. Eventually, steamboats fell victim to railroads, too, but not before they had probed into strange, far-distant places and been involved in many exciting events.

Those Floating Palaces

STEAMBOATS on the Mississippi River became larger, faster, and so ornate during the middle of the 1800s that the most lordly of them were called floating palaces. Compared to the simple, small houses that most Americans of the time lived in, the swift passenger packets on the Mississippi and Ohio rivers had a palatial appearance. In fact, when praising the elegance of a friend's home, visitors sometimes exclaimed, "It's just like a steamboat!"

The riverboats also had a nasty habit of exploding when their boilers overheated, running aground during seasons of low water, and bursting into flames because of their flimsy wooden construction. Going aboard one of these romantic-looking vessels for a trip on the river was exciting in more ways than one.

Usually, the boats were taller than the buildings ashore. As a rule they had four decks. Near water level, the main deck housed boilers, engines, firewood, freight, and cheap-fare passengers. Above it was the boiler deck, with the finest cabins, and still higher was the hurricane deck. On top of that came the shorter Texas deck, mostly for cabins of the boat's crew. Topping all of these was the lofty pilothouse, glassed in on all four sides. Higher still rose the twin smokestacks.

It is no wonder that passengers who entered the main public cabin on the boiler deck exclaimed in awe. In the largest steamboats, this cabin was as long as a football field and two stories high. Since it was so long and less than twenty feet wide, the cabin resembled a gaily decorated tunnel. Sunshine filtered down through the stained-glass skylights onto richly patterned carpeting. Chandeliers of sparkling glass hung from the ceiling, shedding a flickering light from their oil lamps at night onto the white uniforms of the waiters and the linen tablecloths. Along each side, rows of pillars formed corridors; from these corridors, doors led into the private sleeping cabins. On each door was an oil painting and a doorknob of porcelain or glass, a symbol of elegance. The cabins also had a second door, leading out directly onto the deck.

Across the ceiling of the public cabin were crisscross wooden beams of elaborate scrollwork. The entire cabin usually was painted white, trimmed with gold leaf. A huge mirror at one end, reflecting all this glory, made the cabin seem even longer than its actual three hundred feet. This mirror was in the ladies' cabin, as the back portion of the far-reaching tunnel was called. At the other end gleamed a gigantic sterling silver drinking-water dispenser, whose silver drinking cups were chained in place to foil souvenir hunters. Since steamboats were designed high at the ends and low in the middle, passengers actually walked downhill from each end of the cabin to its center.

A typical scene as a steamboat ties up at a landing to discharge and take aboard passengers and freight.

Imagine the impression such magnificence had on rustic passengers who came aboard from their primitive frontier farms! More worldly travelers often found this elaborately contrived splendor too pretentious, however. Sneeringly, they referred to the frills and curlicues of the jigsaw scrollwork as "steamboat Gothic." The phrase still is heard occasionally to describe decorations that are too ornate.

Other travelers were more disturbed about the miserable safety records the steamboats had. There was, for example, the old fellow from Arkansas whom Hodding Carter quotes in his book, *Lower Mississippi*. This backwoodsman in a coonskin cap was aboard an upriver steamboat that had to stop for repairs. He left the boat in disgust. He'd had enough.

"This is the last time I ever mean to put my foot in one of these contrivances," he announced. "I have been five times run high and dry on a sand bank, four times snagged, three times sawyered, and twice blown up sky-high. I calculate I have given these creatures a pretty fair trial and darn my britches if I ever trust my carcass in one again. Take care of my plunder. I will call for it in St. Louis."

Perhaps he had suffered more than his share of bad luck on the boats. Or perhaps he was exaggerating to emphasize his point. The fact is that more than four thousand people were killed or injured in accidents to steamboats on the Mississippi between 1816 and 1850.

There wasn't much for passengers to do except watch the shores go by, talk, sew, read, or play cards. And eat. How they did eat on the finest boats! Tables were set in the long cabin for each meal, and elaborate printed menus were distributed from which passengers could choose their food. One typical printed menu that has survived lists sixteen different desserts, plus ice cream!

Meanwhile, down on the main deck, the cheap-ticket passengers ate whatever cold food they had brought from home, or cooked simple meals on a stove that was permitted on some boats. No printed menus or hand-painted china for them! Not even beds.

They slept fully dressed, or tried to sleep, on the deck or wherever they could curl up in a corner among the stacks of freight. When three hundred or more "deckers" were jammed together on a boat, enduring the heat from the boilers and the oily stench and noise of the engines, their discomfort was intense.

Although passengers were aboard a boat for several days on many trips, little effort was made by the management to entertain them, except for an occasional amateur theatrical or musical performance in the main cabin at night. A writer for *The New York Times* who made a Mississippi voyage in 1860 told about one of these.

"We had a grand concert on the boat this evening, given by the barber, waiters, and cooks. It was patronized by governors, colonels, honorables, and generals without end."

In the midst of the harmonizing and applause, an unscheduled excitement broke up the show: "The cry of 'Man overboard!' started us all from our seats and sent a thrill indescribable through every person present."

A man rowing across the river in the darkness had been hit by the boat's bow, sucked under, and was not found. Such a tragedy is not surprising, because not until years later did the steamboats have searchlights or bright running lights to illuminate them during night voyaging.

The grandest of all the Mississippi steamboats, it is generally agreed, was the splendid *J.M. White III*. She was built after the Civil War, in 1878, at a time when the railroads were drawing passengers and freight cargoes away from the riverboats. The builders believed that with a boat of exceptional speed and splendor they could recapture some of this lost trade.

What a glorious vessel she was! The cabin was illuminated by twelve chandeliers, whose beams fell on tables set with fine china bearing the boat's picture and monogram. The carpet for the cabin, 265 feet long by 19 feet wide, was woven in Europe as a single enormous piece. Around the cabin stood walnut sofas with velvet upholstery. The side wheels were nearly as tall as a four-story building, the twin smokestacks were so big that a man could walk

The long, ornate cabin of the Great Republic *in this 1872 photograph is an example of the elaborate furnishings on Mississippi River packets. Notice the intricate carpet and the sterling silver water container on the table in the foreground.*

through them if they were laid horizontally. There were twelve boilers to produce power for the engines, which together generated 3200 horsepower. Up in the pilothouse, the steering wheel was eleven feet wide. The deep-toned bell on the hurricane deck weighed nearly a ton and a half; and the giant whistle didn't merely blow a loud blast, it bellowed a five-tone chord.

Alas, much of the time the *J.M. White III* sailed half empty. Magnificent as she was, the boat was a financial failure and doomed to a relatively short life. After eight years of sailing, she caught fire at a landing in Louisiana. There was a cargo of gunpowder in the hold. When the flames licked through the wooden hull and reached the gunpowder, a thunderous explosion ripped the boat into hundreds of pieces. As years passed, the remnants of the *J.M. White III* were covered by the heavy burden of mud the Mississippi's waters carried downstream.

During the grand days of steamboating, most steamboats on the lower Mississippi River and many on the Ohio were side paddle-wheelers; they were more maneuverable and faster than stern-wheelers. Boats that traveled on the upper Mississippi, on lesser rivers, and up the long, twisting length of the Missouri River more often were stern-wheelers, because they could run in even shallower water than the side-wheelers. The only major advantage of the stern-wheeler was its pushing power. In later decades when passenger traffic on the lower Mississippi diminished and more boats pushed freight barges, the stern-wheeler type became commonplace there, too. The screw propeller used on ocean-going ships wouldn't work on the inland rivers. It bit too deep under water.

Piloting steamboats through the treacherous shoals and bends of the Mississippi, and past the lurking snags, required enormous skill. Pilots were the kings of the river. Their authority was unlimited. Even the captain of a boat could not tell a pilot what to do, when it came to navigating, although the captain might be a part-owner of the vessel. If a pilot decided that a boat should tie up on shore for the night, he announced his decision and the captain had to accept it.

Old prints of steamboat explosions show the difference between a side-wheeler and a stern-wheeler.

During the steamboat era, the Mississippi was an ever changing river. Its banks eroded and landmarks by which pilots steered were wiped out. No buoys or warning lights marked the channel. The current shifted and cut new channels behind points of land in the river's meandering course. New islands appeared in the stream, created when floating debris and silt piled up around a submerged tree or piece of steamboat wreckage. To the pilot, every trip up or down stream meant a fresh challenge to his skill and memory. The few charts of the river's course that existed were almost useless because they became out of date so quickly. In those pre-electronic times, no automatic equipment told the pilot the depth of the river or warned him of obstacles. He kept his boat afloat and moving by memorizing every quirk of the river and reading the telltale signs on the water's surface; these he learned to identify through experience.

To the untrained passenger's eye, the ripples and fanlike clusters of lines on the surface of the water were pretty bits of scenery. To the pilot, they meant danger: shallow reefs or hidden trees lurking beneath the surface. A floating log showed that the river was rising. This was important for the pilot to know, because in a rising river the water was higher in the middle of the stream than at the edges, and that caused a boat to drift toward the banks. A faint dimple in the current told the pilot that a rock or piece of wreckage lay in wait beneath it. Lines or circles on patches of slick water indicated that a shoal was building up on the river bottom.

The pilot knew that every point of land jutting into a stream had a sandbar leading out from it, formed by the swing of the current. All these things, and a thousand more, were an essential part of the Mississippi pilot's knowledge, and they could not be learned from books. In order to "read" these signs at night, the pilot needed blackness around him; at nightfall screens were placed around the fireboxes and coverings over the cabin skylights.

Behind the steering wheel and pilot's seat in the glassed-in pilot-house was a long bench. Here sat other pilots, traveling free of charge between assignments. They were "watching the river"—

Off-duty steamboatmen gathered in the pilothouse to "study the river" and exchange yarns while watching the steersman maneuver through hazards in the stream.

that is, keeping up to date on the changes in its channel and distinguishing marks, so they would be freshly informed when they next piloted a boat. Yarn-spinning among the men went on endlessly. So did discreet second-guessing about how the pilot in command maneuvered through the trouble spots.

Samuel Clemens became a licensed pilot on the Mississippi in the 1850s after serving an apprenticeship under Horace Bixby, a famous riverman. Clemens took his renowned pen name, Mark Twain, from a call shouted by men who stood on a boat's main deck and tossed a lead-weighted line overboard to determine how deep the river was at that point. "Twain" is an old-fashioned word for "two." When the leadsman's marked line showed a water depth of twelve feet, he called out, "Mark twain," meaning two fathoms. A fathom is six feet.

In his book of reminiscences, *Life on the Mississippi*, Clemens described a critical moment on the river one night when the steam-boat that Bixby was piloting, with young Clemens as his "cub," had to pass through a shallow place around a bend of the river in darkness.

Mr. Bixby pulled the cord, and two deep, mellow notes from the big bell floated off on the night. Then a pause, and one more note was struck. The watchman's voice followed, from the hurricane-deck:

"Labboard lead, there! Stabboard lead!"

The cries of the leadmen began to rise out of the distance, and were gruffly repeated by the word-passers on the hurricane-deck.

"M-a-r-k three! M-a-r-k three! Quarter-less-three! Half twain! Quarter twain! M-a-r-k twain! Quarter-less—"

Mr. Bixby pulled two bell-ropes, and was answered by faint jinglings far below in the engine-room, and our speed slackened.

With a skilled touch on the wheel, Bixby got the boat over the first reef. In the darkness an especially black spot appeared ahead, an island near which the boat must pass as it attempted to cross a hidden sandbar.

The water grew shoaler and shoaler, by the leadman's cries, till it was down to:

"Eight-and-a-half! E-i-g-h-t feet! E-i-g-h-t feet! Seven-and—"

Mr. Bixy said warningly through his speaking-tube to the engineer:

"Stand by, now!"

"Ay, ay, sir!"

"Seven-and-a-half! Seven feet! *Six*-and—"

We touched bottom! Instantly Mr. Bixby set a lot of bells ringing, shouted through the tube, "*Now*, let her have it—every ounce you've got!" then to his partner, "Put her hard down! snatch her! snatch her!" The boat rasped and ground her way through the sand, hung upon the apex of disaster a single tremendous instant, and then over she went! And such a shout as went up at Mr. Bixby's back never loosened the roof of a pilot-house before.

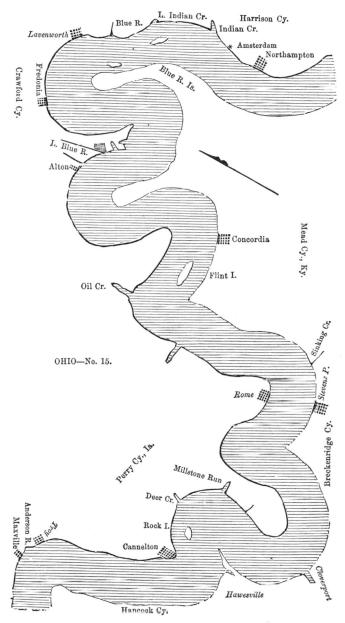

This map of a twisting portion of the Ohio River shows some of the problems a steamboat pilot faced in maneuvering his vessel.

When the Mississippi and Ohio overflowed their banks with floodwaters caused by runoff from the northern winter snows and the spring rains, steamboat pilots could steer their vessels on short-cuts over land that was dry most of the year. By following a floodwater channel that cut across the base of a big bend, a daring pilot could save fifteen or twenty miles from the normal route around the point, about an hour's sailing time. If he didn't hang the boat up on a snag or rip out its bottom, that is.

Quite the opposite situation existed during the months of low water. Running aground was a constant danger. In portions of the river known for their sandbars, the usual practice of taking depth measurements with a line dropped from the boat as it moved wasn't good enough. In dangerous waters, pilots often used a method called "sounding."

The big steamboat tied up on shore, although to the casual eye the water ahead looked quite normal. An off-duty pilot and a crew rowed ahead in a small yawl to hunt for the best water. From the pilothouse, the pilot in charge watched them through a spyglass; his higher position gave him a better perspective. Occasionally he blew the whistle in prearranged signals, meaning that the searchers should try in different directions from where they were. When the rowboat reached the underwater barrier, the pilot aboard it probed the bottom with a long pole until he found the deepest spot, the place where the steamboat had the best chance of slipping across. A crewman tossed a buoy overboard to mark the spot. This was a simple device, a long piece of wood weighed with a rock tied to it with a rope. Often the buoy was an old-fashioned wooden school bench. If the maneuver was being done at night, a paper lantern with a lighted candle was placed on the buoy, giving off a glimmer of guiding light.

The rowers raised their oars straight up, as a signal to the pilot. He acknowledged "O.K." with a toot of the whistle. Then the vessel crept forward, nosing straight at the buoy.

Passengers lined the rails to watch the critical moment. They were curious, and more than a little anxious; if the boat stuck on the sandbar, it might need hours or even days to get off and their trips would be delayed.

As the prow neared the buoy, the pilot ordered full steam ahead. With a crunch, the hull rode straight over the makeshift buoy, ground its way through the sand, and emerged safely on the other side of the bar. Or if the pilot's luck was bad, it became stuck. Travel by steamboat was full of such gambles and uncertainties, even on the mighty Mississippi. On the lesser rivers where steamboats poked their noses, the odds against an undelayed, uneventful trip were far higher. The garish posters announcing sailing schedules of river steamboats never mentioned the possibility of such delays, but they happened frequently.

When a boat became stuck, the passengers could expect to be ordered ashore, along with the freight, to lighten the vessel during efforts to free it. Indeed, captains tended to treat their low-fare deck passengers almost as impersonally as they did their freight cargoes. They were especially negligent toward the impoverished Irish and German immigrants who crowded the lower decks of boats upbound from New Orleans, to which they had come aboard immigrant ships from Europe. In one notorious incident, the captain of a boat stuck on a Mississippi sandbar ordered a hundred German immigrants onto a midstream island in freezing weather. Thus lightened, the boat was able to slide across the bar—and then sailed right on, leaving the immigrants stranded on the island without food or supplies, miles from the nearest community.

Twice a day, sometimes more, the pilot of a steamboat sounded three bells to announce a landing, not to take on or discharge passengers and freight, but to bring aboard a fresh stack of wood for the boilers. During the first forty years or so of Mississippi steamboating, almost all boats used wood for fuel. After the Civil War, coal was burned by many.

Huge amounts of wood were consumed by the boats, but for many years the dense forests along the Mississippi and the Ohio supplied all that was needed. As farmers cleared their land so they could plant crops, they cut the felled trees into four-foot lengths

The cotton crop of the South was all important to Northern and overseas mills.

for sale. When a boat stopped at a wood-loading station, roustabouts of the deck crew formed a continuous line, carrying cut wood from the shore and piling it around the boilers. Deck passengers helped sometimes, in return for a reduction in their fares. Going upstream, a captain, instead of having wood carried up the gangplank, had a loaded wood barge lashed alongside his boat. As the vessel sailed ahead, roustabouts transferred the logs from barge to steamboat. This saved important time for the fast passenger boats trying to keep a schedule. When the barge was empty, it was cast loose to drift downstream to the loading station.

Relatively few of the steamboats were fast, sleek, elaborate craft like those we have been talking about, but they were the ones which received most attention. One of these, the *Grand Republic*, was famous not only for her ornate furnishings but because her owners advertised her as the "calendar boat." Her dimensions, they said, were exactly those of the calendar—365 feet long (days in a year), 52 feet wide (the weeks), 12-foot hull depth (the months), and 7 decks high (days in a week). It was a catchy claim, but not quite true, as boatyard workers discovered when the boat was rebuilt. They measured her and found that she actually was only 350 feet long.

Hundreds of other steamboats were slow plodders, shabbily built and often dirty, that made money for their owners by hauling whatever cargoes and passengers they could pick up at obscure towns and plantation landings. Passengers sometimes were lured aboard by signs of imminent sailing activity, only to find after they had purchased tickets that the boat wouldn't leave until its captain had found more cargo to put aboard.

On the lower Mississippi, cotton was the most important cargo. Much of it was shipped to New Orleans for transfer to ocean-going ships bound for Europe and England. Since cotton was bulky, packaged in large rectangular bales, boats that carried it usually were built with wide guards, flat extensions of the main deck that stuck far out from the hull on each side, over the water. Cotton bales were stacked high on these guards. Balancing the load was essential. If too many bales were put on one side, the boat would capsize. The all-time record load of cotton was carried by the *Henry Frank* in the 1870s—9226 bales stacked all the way up to the pilothouse. These walls of cotton blocked out the daylight for

Cotton bales delivered to ports by riverboats were often transferred to ocean-going steamships.

The largest load of cotton ever carried on a steamboat is shown as the Henry Frank *arrived at New Orleans in 1881 with 9226 bales. The unfortunate passengers aboard had their view blocked completely.*

the frustrated passengers, who must have felt cheated as they sat in the dark, unable to see the shores.

Up and down the river, too, went another kind of vessel, the showboat. These floating theaters, which usually were barges pushed by small steamboats, stopped at the small river towns in the mornings. The actors, crew—everybody aboard—put on a parade along the main street. At night the local residents, hungry for entertainment in their isolated communities, flocked aboard the showboat.

While most showboat casts presented regular plays, vaudeville, or circus acts, others cheated the audiences by turning the shows into sales talks for useless patent medicines. One unscrupulous but ingenious showman managed to do both. On the stage at one end of the roofed-over barge, the actors put on a play in which the sickly looking heroine wandered from place to place hunting a medicine to cure her illness. The villain tried to deceive her and keep her away from the cure she sought. But the hero arrived just in time to give her a magical remedy from the medicine bottle he carried. The villain was foiled, and in the final scene the heroine appeared fresh, healthy, and beautiful.

The curtain closed. Out from behind it stepped the captain of the steamboat, holding a bottle of medicine aloft.

"Here it is, folks. The wonderful medicine that made our little heroine healthy and pretty!" he proclaimed. "It will do the same thing for you. This is your opportunity to buy this magic elixir. Fifty cents a bottle—three for a dollar!"

Swept away by the excitement of the show and the captain's sales talk, many gullible persons in the audience bought bottles. They didn't know that each bottle contained water from their river, with coloring added after the mud had been strained out.

Often the showboats played heart-tugging melodramas such as *East Lynne, Ten Nights in a Bar Room,* and *Bertha the Sewing Machine Girl.* The actors emoted with exaggerated gestures, and the audiences loved it. They became so involved emotionally that they believed the action on the stage was real. One night in a West Virginia port, a miner in the audience became so furious at the way the villain was attempting to harm the heroine that he jumped onto the stage, grabbed the dastardly fellow, and threw him overboard.

As the drenched and dripping actor could testify when he climbed back aboard, you never could be sure what would happen on the riverboats.

Showboats like the Goldenrod *brought entertainment to residents along the Mississippi and Ohio rivers. The plays and vaudeville acts they presented brightened the lives of those who lived in isolated riverfront towns.*

CHAPTER SEVEN

Races and Wrecks

RARELY if ever had the levee at New Orleans been so crowded as it was that afternoon. For more than a mile along the shore, tall stacks of steamboats, scores of them, poured smoke into the sky until it formed a cloud that spread over the city. Roustabouts tossed gummy pitch pine into the fireboxes, to make the smoke blacker and thicker. Everywhere there was evidence of last-minute preparation as boats went through the daily ritual of departing up the Mississippi. Passengers hurried aboard. Freight was stacked on the main decks.

Traditionally, steamboats sailed from New Orleans between 4:00 and 5:00 P.M. in a stately parade punctuated with a chorus of bells and whistles. Today was special, however. Spectators milled along the water's edge, chattering with excitement. Many could be seen making bets with each other, some of them big money wagers of five hundred dollars or more.

The throng's attention centered on two boats that were nosed into the levee two berths apart. They were spacious craft, gleaming white side-wheelers known up and down the Mississippi for their speed and endurance; their names widely recognized around the United States, and in Europe, too, because of the rivalry between them to be the speed queen of the river.

One was the *Robert E. Lee*, the other was the *Natchez*. They

Preparations for sailing at New Orleans. Traditionally, the steamboats sailed away from the wharf in a stately parade.

were about to test their speed for 1200 miles up to St. Louis in the most famous steamboat race in history. News of the impending contest had created intense interest on both sides of the Atlantic Ocean. Bulletins reporting their progress were to be telegraphed and cabled wherever the wires went. Betting odds on the race were posted on the stock exchanges of New York, Paris, and Vienna. Steamboat racing long had been known as a daredevil, headlong competition in which rivals tossed aside caution—indeed, good sense—and risked blowing themselves to bits by overstraining their boilers to squeeze out the last ounce of speed. Here was the most controversial, most highly publicized race of them all.

The actual prize for victory was simple enough—a pair of gilded deer antlers. "Holding the antlers" was the honor given to the fastest boat on the river. As the racers gathered steam that afternoon of June 30, 1870, the *Natchez* under Captain Thomas P. Leathers held the antlers. Captain John W. Cannon of the *Robert E. Lee* was determined to take them away. Victory meant far more than the antlers, however; prestige and money were at stake, because passengers loved to say that they traveled on the fastest boat on the river.

The Robert E. Lee *gets up steam for departure from a Mississippi River levee. She was the fastest boat on the river.*

Precisely at one minute before 5:00 P.M., the *Robert E. Lee* rang her bell and began to back out from the wharf at the foot of Canal Street. Her reversed paddle wheels churned the water and steam hissed from her exhaust pipes.

"There goes the *Lee,*" was the shout up and down the waterfront.

The boat rounded to and pointed her nose upstream. As she did so, she fired her gun to mark her official starting time.

Four minutes passed—it seemed far longer than that to her supporters—before the *Natchez* got under way and fired her gun. First advantage to the *Lee.*

The pilots of other steamboats going on routine trips kept their vessels well to the side, while passengers cheered the racers.

That four-minute difference continued during the first hours. At Ten-Mile Point above New Orleans, the *Lee* led by three and a half minutes. At Twenty-Four Mile Point, she was four minutes and forty seconds in front. Some 1175 miles of twisting, treacherous river remained before the finish line at St. Louis. Gradually the *Robert E. Lee* pulled ahead. Although the boats appeared to be

90

evenly matched, Captain Cannon of the *Lee* had stripped his boat for action, removing anything that might create a drag on her speed, even the doors, and refusing to carry freight or passengers on the trip. Captain Leathers of the *Natchez* made fewer special preparations and had both freight and passengers aboard.

Both boats had brought along many slabs of spoiled bacon, to be thrown into their furnace fires on top of the burning coal. Bacon grease made the fires burn hotter and generate more steam. The firemen also used barrels of resin, tallow candles, and pine knots, which had the same effect. Flames and showers of sparks flashed from the tops of the smokestacks as the rivals sped along.

A correspondent of the New Orleans *Picayune*, traveling aboard the *Natchez*, told how the race appeared to a participant:

"The scene from the time of departure till dark last evening baffles description. As we steamed along the watery track, the whole country on both sides of the river seemed alive with a strange excitement, expressed in a variety of gestures, the waving of handkerchiefs and hats, and running along the shore as if to encourage the panting steamer; and now and then far-off shouts came cheeringly over the waters, and were plainly heard above the roaring of the fires, the clatter of machinery, the splashing of the water, and the escape of steam."

The *Natchez* never caught up. Slowly she fell farther behind.

The gilded antlers held by the *Natchez* before this race had been fastened onto the wharfboat at her namesake city, with a printed explanation of how she had won them.

As the *Robert E. Lee* raced past the Natchez wharfboat, Captain Cannon shouted to the wharfmaster from his hurricane deck, "Take those antlers down!"

At Memphis, interest in the race was so intense that businesses shut down, schools were closed, and hundreds of excursion boats and small craft carried spectators downstream to welcome the racers. The *Robert E. Lee* passed the city one hour and two minutes ahead. Her lead was still greater at Cairo, where the Ohio River branches off. Above that city the *Natchez*, already trailing con-

An artist's conception of the famous steamboat race in which the Robert
E. Lee *defeated the* Natchez *over a 1200-mile course from New Orleans
to St. Louis. Actually, the boats seldom were close together.*

siderably, was delayed by engine trouble. Both boats had to sail
through fog for awhile. The *Robert E. Lee* pulled across the finish
line at St. Louis the victor by three hours and forty-five minutes.
She had raced upstream the approximately twelve hundred miles
from New Orleans in three days, eighteen hours, and fourteen
minutes at an average of fourteen miles an hour, including stops,
the fastest speed ever recorded by a paddle-wheeler on that route.

Yet the *Robert E. Lee*'s victory, decisive as it seems, stirred up
an argument—inevitably, perhaps, since so many millions of dollars
had been wagered on the result. Fairly early in the race, when the
Lee needed more fuel, by prearrangement Captain Cannon had
another steamboat, the *Frank Paragoud*, tie on alongside the *Lee*
and transfer a hundred tons of pine knots to the *Lee*'s deck as they
steamed along together. Supporters of the *Natchez* cried, "Unfair!"
They contended that the *Frank Paragoud* not only gave the *Robert
E. Lee* a refueling advantage but used her engines to help the racer.
Even that help, for whatever it was worth, wasn't considered by
most people to be enough to wipe out the *Lee*'s victory, however.

Unlike this renowned contest, most steamboat racing was on a
more impromptu basis, when two boats happened to find themselves side by side and their masters decided to test each other.

An amusing account of such a spur-of-the-moment race appears in the diary of Charles Francis Adams, Jr., who was a passenger aboard the *Alhambra* coming down the Mississippi from St. Paul, Minnesota, in 1860. About two o'clock in the morning, the *Alhambra* happened to be almost alongside the *Winona*, another sternwheeler. Neither boat had much speed, but they were evenly matched.

Through the darkness they raced in low water, nose to nose, battling to get ahead of each other before the channel narrowed. At times, thirty or forty feet of water flowed between them, then they were almost side by side.

Adams described what happened: "Finally the channel apparently narrowed, and the interval was closed rapidly up, until, with a bump, the two boats collided heavily, almost throwing me from my feet. The guards seemed to groan and tremble, but neither boat gave, and so the two rushed along with rubbing sides. I suddenly found myself standing face to face with a passenger on the other boat, and somewhat apparently to his surprise, extended my hand, and wished him good morning.

"He shook my hand, remarking that he proposed to leave us; and so on the two boats went.

"I think we must have rushed along in this way for several minutes; but, finally, they shouldered us out of the channel, and, giving a triumphant whistle, shot ahead and down the river, leaving us to follow."

Not until 1852, after steamboats had been sailing for more than thirty years, did the federal government have an effective safety law for the boats, including boiler inspections. Often racers took foolhardy risks, especially in the pre-inspection days. Captains ordered the safety valves on the boilers weighted shut, to create greater steam pressure and more speed, at the risk of having the boilers explode.

About thirty miles above Memphis one day, the *Brandywine* and the *Hudson* had hooked up in a race. The *Brandywine* was trailing, and her captain had ordered resin poured into the fires. Sparks from the stack ignited a deckload of carriage wheels packed in straw.

Three steamboats race along the Ohio River, two of them almost neck to neck. Crewmen tossed highly combustible materials into the boiler fires to generate extra power while racing.

Hurriedly the crew tossed the cargo overboard, but it was too late, because the boat's woodwork caught fire in the strong wind. The pilot's attempt to take the boat to shore failed when the vessel struck an offshore sandbar. More than a hundred persons perished in the fire or from drowning as they tried to swim ashore.

Traveling on steamboats could be dangerous even when they weren't racing. The list of boats destroyed by fire, collision, explosion, or by hitting obstacles grew longer and longer, until, by the time the 1852 safety law was adopted, 420 steamboats had been wrecked on the western rivers, about half of them by explosions. One compilation listed 932 people killed in steamboat explosions on the Mississippi between 1816 and 1848, and 511 killed on the Ohio. Because passengers wanted speed, captains found ways to sneak around the safety rules, and even a well-intentioned law couldn't prevent shipboard fires when the boats were built of wood. A traveler in 1837 counted twenty-five wrecked steamboats between Cairo and St. Louis.

Hundreds of thousands of dollars in gold and coins being held in boat safes or carried by passengers vanished in steamboat explosions and fires. Presumably this treasure still lies in the mud of the river bottoms, although some probably has been swept out to sea by the current.

When an airliner takes off today, a hostess explains to the passengers how to use the safety equipment and points out location of the exits, in case of an emergency. No such advice was given to steamboat passengers. Experienced travelers learned a few tricks to improve their odds for survival. Some of this wisdom was included in an article in *Frank Leslie's Monthly* in 1881 headed, "How to Jump From a Steamer in Case of Accident." It said:

"It is worth while for persons who travel on steamboats to know

An artist depicted men and women passengers escaping from a burning steamboat. Some grabbed floating bales of cotton and debris, while others climbed into a rowboat at the vessel's side.

and remember that they have little chance of escaping with their lives if, in the event of an accident, they leap into the water in front of the paddlewheels while the wheels are in motion. In spite of their efforts they will be drawn close to the side of the vessel, and suffer a blow from the wheel, which will either kill them outright or disable them so that they can no longer help themselves. They should leap from behind the wheels if possible, when they find it necessary to take to the water . . .

"In cases where communication with the after parts of the vessel is cut off by flame, it is best to remain on the boat as long as possible, and, if forced to take to the water, to plunge headlong. Persons diving in that manner do not come to the surface as soon as they would if they descended to the same depth dropping feet first; and they go deeper with the same effort, unless they have trained themselves to hold the limbs entirely rigid, descend perpendicularly and not move hands or feet until they begin to rise."

These instructions for survival helped men, no doubt, but what about a woman in a hoop skirt or a bustle? Her chances of making a deep dive while wearing such a billowing garment were remote, indeed.

The fate of one young woman passenger in a steamboat fire who didn't dare dive into the water was described in a book published in 1856, *Lloyd's Steamboat Directory and Disasters on the Western Waters*. A young man, Mr. Mann, and a young woman, Miss Sherman, were strolling rather romantically arm in arm on the upper deck of the *Erie* when flames swept up from below. Gallantly, Mr. Mann ripped a plank from a bench, intending to throw it overboard so Miss Sherman could float on it until picked up.

"But new difficulties presented themselves," James T. Lloyd, the author, wrote in his flowery prose. "No persuasions could induce Miss Sherman to descend to the water. In these embarrassing circumstances, he placed one end of the board over the railing at the stern; Miss Sherman was seated on the projecting extremity, and Mr. Mann earnestly entreated some men who were clustered around the rudder post, to assist him in lowering the plank and the young

Old print shows the burning of the Erie.

lady to the water, but no attention was paid to his entreaties. Miss Sherman in the meanwhile, being made dizzy by her frightful position, fell from the plank, sunk in the river, and was seen no more."

Luckier than poor Miss Sherman was a feminine passenger of another burning steamboat, the *Georgia*. Lloyd reported, "A woman who fell or leaped from the cabin floor to the main deck was caught on the horns of an infuriated ox, and thereby received several severe wounds, but the animal threw her into the water and she was saved."

Tragic stories of steamboat boiler blasts abound. Among the most graphic was the fate of the *Moselle*, a fast boat only a month old, on the Ohio River. She came steaming down around a bend near Cincinnati on the afternoon of April 25, 1838, a fine-looking craft with an American flag fluttering at her stern. Crowded aboard her were hundreds of immigrants from Europe, headed to the West.

The Moselle *exploding in the Ohio River as she pulls away from a landing near Cincinnati in 1838*

At a landing place near Cincinnati, two families of Germans had signaled the *Moselle* ashore to pick them up and carry them to St. Louis.

Perhaps the *Moselle*'s captain was a bit irritated at having to stop, because he was trying to catch up with the rival *Tribune*, which had left Cincinnati an hour earlier. In any case, the engineer did not ease off the steam pressure during the brief halt. The two families hustled up the gangplank in a hurry. The captain rang the bell for departure. Instead of pulling the boat slowly out into the current before speeding up, the pilot signaled for full speed ahead. The *Moselle* drew out from the bank a few yards; then, without warning, blew up with an ear-shattering roar. Timber splinters, doors, jagged fragments of boiler iron, cargo, and bodies were hurled into the air through billowing clouds of torrid steam. A section of one boiler blew six hundred feet and smashed in the end of a building. One victim landed on the roof of a house, falling through it. The explosive force was so tremendous that the body of the pilot was blown all the way across the river onto the Kentucky shore. Not a trace was ever found of the two German families who had stepped aboard moments earlier. Many of the victims were scalded by water escaping from the boilers.

The wonder was that anyone survived, but of the nearly 300 persons aboard, 117 did so. More than 150 passengers and crewmen perished.

A committee of inquiry into the tragedy told bitter truths not only about the *Moselle* but about other steamship catastrophes. It reported:

"Such disasters have their foundation in the present mammoth evil of our country, an inordinate love of gain. We are not satisfied with getting rich, but we must get rich in a day. We are not satisfied with traveling at a speed of ten miles an hour, but we must fly. Such is the effect of competition that everything must be done cheap; boiler iron must be cheap, traveling must be done cheap, freight must be cheap, yet everything must be speedy. A steamboat must establish a reputation of a few minutes 'swifter' in a hundred miles than others, before she can make fortunes fast enough to satisfy the owners. Also this seems to be demanded by the blind tyranny of custom, and the common consent of the community."

Of all the disasters on the rivers, the worst occurred at the end of the Civil War, to a passenger boat, the *Sultana*, overloaded with Union soldiers homeward bound after release from Confederate prisons. More people perished when the *Sultana* blew up on the Mississippi River above Memphis than perished when the famous ocean liner *Titanic* hit an iceberg and sank in the Atlantic Ocean. Yet the *Sultana* disaster received less attention than it should have, because it occurred at the time the funeral train of the assassinated Abraham Lincoln was traveling past huge crowds from Washington to the President's burial place at Springfield, Illinois. Millions were grief stricken at the death of Lincoln and could think of little else.

The month of April, 1865, was a momentous one. On the ninth,

This view of New Orleans shows the steamboat Sultana *at left.*

General Robert E. Lee surrendered the main Confederate Army to General Ulysses S. Grant at Appomattox Court House, Virginia. On the night of the fourteenth, President Lincoln was shot while attending a play at Ford's Theater in Washington. The two armies, victors and vanquished, were starting to disband. Emotions and uncertainty were high.

In the midst of all this, the *Sultana* sailed on a routine trip north from New Orleans with passengers and freight. She was a good boat, only two years old; large, but not quite the size of some Mississippi packets. She was licensed to carry 76 cabin passengers, plus 300 deck passengers and crewmen, a total of 376. Among her cabin passengers were a man and his wife who were moving from the South to the North and had seventeen thousand dollars in gold hidden in their stateroom—gold that never has been found.

Shortly before reaching Vicksburg, the *Sultana* had trouble with her boilers. Captain J. Cass Mason had to halt the boat at Vicksburg while a local boilermaker welded a patch onto the side of one boiler. While the *Sultana* was in port, the Army decided that she should carry to the North a throng of Union soldiers from Confederate prisons, including the notorious Andersonville, who had assembled at Vicksburg. Captain Mason welcomed this decision, because the boat was to be paid five dollars for each soldier it carried. But as he watched more and more soldiers marching aboard, he became aghast. The *Sultana* was being dangerously overloaded, he knew, but Army officers ignored his protest.

Happy and laughing at going home, soldiers swarmed all over the boat. They spread blankets wherever they could find space. Nobody knew exactly, but by the best count available the *Sultana* left Vicksburg carrying about 2400 soldiers, 100 civilian passengers, and 80 crewmen, a total of more than 2500. That was nearly seven times as many as safety regulations permitted. The boat even carried a shipment of horses and mules near the stern on her lower deck.

About 1:00 A.M. on April 27, the *Sultana* sailed from Memphis and crossed to the Arkansas shore for coal. As she pulled out from the coaling station in the rainy darkness, almost everyone settled down to sleep as best possible in the overcrowded conditions. Her pilot steered her out into midstream. Because the river was exceptionally broad with the spring rains, the *Sultana* proceeded upstream more than a mile from the Arkansas shore and two miles from the Tennessee shore. She was passing a group of islands about seven miles north of Memphis when her boilers exploded.

Chaos and terror followed. The smokestacks tumbled onto the upper deck and crushed soldiers jammed together there. Pieces of iron from the boilers were hurled through the cabins. Bodies were thrown high in the air. The wooden superstructure caught fire and hissing steam spread along the decks. Many passengers and crewmen were blown overboard, dead or alive. Hundreds more jumped into the river, grabbing any bit of debris that floated by, until the water around the boat was so thick with heads that others had difficulty finding places to jump. Captain Mason stayed with his

In the worst disaster in steamboat history, the heavily overloaded
Sultana *blew up in the Mississippi in 1865.*

boat to the end and was seen tossing wreckage overboard to
floundering survivors.

Some survivors reached shore by hanging onto wreckage or by
swimming. Rescue boats saved others, but the death toll was horrible.
The most reliable count placed the loss of life at 1585. Over eight
hundred men and women were saved. Despite her perilous overload,
the *Sultana* carried no lifeboats and no safety equipment except
cork lifebelts under each bunk in the upper deck cabins. This final
deadly episode of the war years on the river that had seen so much
fighting was caused by carelessness of unforgivable proportions,
just when its victims were rejoicing that peace had come.

CHAPTER EIGHT

Prepare to Ram!

ONE of the weirdest naval battles in American history was fought in the middle of the Mississippi River, at Memphis, Tennessee, during the Civil War. Thousands of spectators watched it from the bluffs of the city.

The two wooden passenger steamboats that led the North's victorious attack were armed with nothing heavier than an infantryman's rifle. In fact, these "warships" didn't even belong to the United States Navy but were commanded by a newly created Army colonel who had never heard a shot fired in anger before. Their crews were civilians recruited from the peacetime riverboats. Yet the victory was so decisive that the Confederate city of Memphis was forced to surrender to the Union.

Nor was this a battle of subtle feints and diversions, the kind of tactics midshipmen study at the United States Naval Academy at Annapolis. This was more like a clash between two herds of elephants, charging head-on at each other.

A river, even one as broad as the Mississippi, hardly seems a suitable setting for a naval clash. Usually we think of such battles taking place in vast open waters, not in a shallow area hemmed in by shores only a few hundred yards apart. However, that was precisely the site of the Battle of the Rams. It was fought in the spring of 1862, the year before General Grant's final success at Vicksburg gave the North control of the entire Mississippi River.

Memphis, Tennessee, was an important Confederate cotton-shipping center. A naval battle there in 1862 forced its surrender to the Union.

In the early months of 1862, the Confederate government still controlled the river from its mouth below New Orleans to a point near the mouth of its great eastern tributary, the Ohio River. The Confederates guarded the river with fortifications at strong points along its shores and had a River Defense Fleet whose assignment was to prevent Union gunboats at St. Louis, Missouri, from coming down the stream.

The battle at Memphis came about because an eminent civilian engineer named Charles Ellet finally was allowed by the government in Washington to test a form of warfare he had been advocating for seven years: using a ship as a battering ram. In the ancient days of the Greeks and Romans, before gunpowder and cannons, battles between sailing ships were fought in this manner. Now that boats were powered by steam and thus much stronger, Ellet argued, one properly equipped with a heavy pointed nose should be able to smash into another vessel, pierce its wooden side, and sink it.

But the Navy Department in Washington ignored him. The pamphlets he wrote, urging that the Navy equip some of its vessels with rams, were brushed aside. High Navy officers chuckled. What did a landsman whose job was building bridges know about fighting at sea? This was in the years just before the Civil War.

When the Confederate states seceded from the Union and set up their own government, however, they adopted Ellet's idea. The leaders of the new Confederate Navy had been in the United States Navy before the brother-against-brother conflict began and had read his proposals. The Confederates rebuilt the captured Union frigate *Merrimac* into a powerful ram called the *Virginia*, which sank numerous Northern ships at Hampton Roads, Virginia. After that success, they put pointed ram noses on two Mississippi River steamboats. These vessels encountered a group of Union ironclad gunboats on the river, sailed directly into their sides, and sank them with their beaks. News of this defeat shocked the Northern naval leaders.

About the same time, Ellet, the staunch Northerner, who had grown tired of being ignored by the United States Navy, wrote to Secretary of War Edwin M. Stanton, whom he knew slightly.

Stanton answered quickly. He authorized Ellet to purchase Ohio River steamboats, convert them into rams, hire civilian boatsmen as crews, and to have the strange flotilla ready "within twenty days." Since the civilian Ellet was to command the force, he needed a rank of some sort. Stanton appointed him a colonel in the Army, but just for the duration of the planned ramming operation.

"The service you are engaged in is peculiar," the Secretary of War wrote to Ellet. Indeed it was! Therefore Colonel Ellet was not placed under the authority of the Navy but was advised to cooperate with it. In other words, the veteran Navy commander of the Union's gunboat flotilla on the Mississippi had no power to tell this amateur newcomer and his unorthodox squadron what to do, even when they sailed side by side along the same river, against the same enemy.

Following his instructions from the Secretary of War, Ellet scrounged up and down the Ohio River for steamboats he could purchase in a hurry. In the river towns he tacked up printed recruiting posters:

MISSISSIPPI MARINE BRIGADE
Soldiering made easy!   No hard marching!
No carrying Knapsacks!
$100 BOUNTY

Altogether, Ellet assembled nine vessels at New Albany, Indiana, of which the most impressive were two large side-wheel packets he bought at Cincinnati, the *Queen of the West* and the *Monarch*. Normally they carried passengers up and down the Ohio. Now they and the other seven vessels—three stern-wheel towboats, another side-wheeler, a stern-wheel packet, and two small tenders—were declared to be warships. An unlikely looking lot of battle craft they were!

Ellet used his engineering knowledge in preparing his boats for war, as best he could in a hurry. He had carpenters fasten boiler iron around the pilothouses, which were alluring targets for enemy gunners. Around the engines they built wooden shields. Braces were added under the flooring of the lower decks as reinforcement against shocks. Most important, Ellet had workmen install heavy timbers jutting forward from the bow of each boat to form a sharp point. This forward edge was sheathed with iron. Otherwise, the boats were just as they had been in peacetime.

Their mission was to destroy Confederate vessels by punching holes in their sides with the projecting rams. If the Union attackers were sunk in the process of clearing the Confederate Defense Fleet from the Mississippi, that was all right. They were expendable.

Ellet wrote to Stanton, "I would not depend upon the steam rams

Colonel Charles Rivers Ellet

for any sustained effort at fighting. I should rely upon the quickness and suddenness of their assault upon the rebel craft. Their prows, I believe, will run through the strongest vessels the enemy can muster. I have provided means for the men to escape and leave the rams to their fate, once they have accomplished their one purpose."

That was precisely the plan the Confederate Navy had for using its ram ships to sink Union vessels.

The commander of the Confederate squadron of eight passenger boats fixed up as rams was a veteran riverboat captain, J. E. Montgomery. The professional officers of the Confederate Navy had little more control over him than the Union Navy did over Ellet. As Montgomery prepared to lead his rams upstream from Memphis, he apparently did not know that Ellet's rams existed. The

Union commanders in turn were unaware that the Confederates had so many rams. Both sides had surprises awaiting them.

So confident was Ellet of his Northern rams' ability to destroy the enemy that he decided against mounting any cannon on them. They were to go into battle unarmed except for six-shooter revolvers and carbines carried by detachments of sharpshooters posted on each boat. Without the weight of cannon and armor, Ellet reasoned, his boats would be faster.

Naval warfare for control of the Mississippi was moving toward a decisive moment. Far to the south, Admiral David Farragut's Union warships attacking from the Gulf of Mexico captured New Orleans and started up the Mississippi. The armored Union gunboat fleet led by Commodore Charles H. Davis sailed downstream from St. Louis to challenge the Confederate fleet based at Memphis.

Here, at last, came Ellet's opportunity to prove his theory. His rag-tag collection of slightly converted riverboats was ordered into action. The Secretary of War instructed them to steam down the Ohio to Cairo, Illinois, where that river flows into the Mississippi, and join the five Union gunboats. At the rendezvous, Ellet found Davis reluctant to attack. After waiting for several days, Ellet became impatient. He notified both the Secretary of War and Davis that he was going to attack the Confederate fleet immediately with his unarmed boats. Davis reluctantly decided to put the gunboats into action, too.

A chilly mist hung low over the river on the morning of June 6, 1862. Despite the poor visibility, citizens of Memphis gathered on the high ground of their city, knowing that the Confederate fleet was going out after the approaching Union gunboats. Clouds of smoke curled from the stacks of the eight Confederate vessels as they pulled out into the stream in rough formation shortly after dawn. Bales of cotton stacked on their decks provided some protection from small gunfire and earned these vessels their nickname, "cottonclads."

The Northern gunboats approached Memphis from the north until they were about two miles from the Confederate rams. Ellet brought his two best steamboat rams downstream from a position behind the Union gunboats until his command boat, the *Queen of the West*, was alongside the commanding Union gunboat, the *Benton*. A few hundred feet behind the *Queen* waited the *Monarch*, the ram commanded by Ellet's younger brother and assistant, Alfred. The rest of Ellet's boats were drawn up a short distance upstream.

As he was about to step aboard the *Benton* for a talk with the Navy commander, Ellet heard a boom from the advancing Confederate boats. A shell whined overhead. Here was an unpleasant surprise! The Confederate rams carried cannon, which had opened fire on the Northerners.

The two fleets steamed ahead, and as they did so became increasingly visible to each other, despite the veil of gunsmoke and the black smokestack outpourings that mingled over the water. Mist still obscured the Arkansas shore of the river, but the bluffs of Memphis on the east stood out in the growing daylight.

Ellet ordered his *Queen of the West* to charge full force toward the leading Confederate ram, the *General Lovell*. Standing high on the hurricane deck, he waved his sword and shouted through a megaphone to his brother on the nearby *Monarch*: "Come ahead, Alfred!"

Perhaps that wasn't the way a Navy commander would give formal orders, but it worked. Alfred brought the *Monarch* forward close behind the *Queen*. With their paddle wheels churning frantically, the two Union rams suddenly sped ahead of the gunboats, straight at the Confederate rams. Union gunboats lobbed shells downstream toward the Southern boats.

The Union rams had the advantage of traveling downstream. Pushed by the current, they steamed forward at twenty miles an hour. The Confederates were slower, but they were able to rake the Northerners with cannon fire.

Barely a hundred yards separated the *Queen of the West* and the leading Confederate ram, the *General Lovell*. Every second that passed saw the intervening space narrowed, as the jutting prows of

The naval battle in the Mississippi at Memphis between Union and Confederate river fleets in 1862, in which Union passenger steamboats converted into rams led the victorious assault. In this artist's conception, sailors are shown jumping overboard from the stern of a Confederate boat after it was run down by a Union ram.

the two boats pointed straight at each other. The *Monarch* was close behind the *Queen of the West*, and on the Confederate side the *Jeff Thompson* was only a few yards behind the *General Lovell*.

The *Queen* and the *General Lovell* smashed together with a tearing, crunching blow. Both boats shuddered from the impact. At the last second, the current had forced the prow of the Confederate vessel slightly to the left. As a result, the *Queen*'s beak struck the *Lovell* about twenty feet from her bow. Water poured through the *Lovell*'s side, and she sank. Her tall smokestacks and upper passenger deck remained visible while her hull rested on the river bottom. Her crew jumped overboard and tried to swim to shore under heavy small arms fire. For a few moments it looked as though the *Queen of the West* would be dragged to the bottom by the sunken *General Lovell*, but Ellet shook his boat free. Moments later, the *Beauregard* of the Confederate fleet rammed into the left-side paddle wheel of the *Queen of the West* and knocked her out of action. Wounded by a gunshot in the knee. Ellet succeeded in beaching his boat on the Tennessee shore. A torrent of gunfire poured from the guns of both fleets. To the crowds watching from the bluffs, the battle was a melee of explosions, fires, churned-up water, floating debris, and struggling boats.

Out in midstream, Alfred Ellet's *Monarch* and the Confederate *Jeff Thompson* headed toward a nose-to-nose collision like two clumsy giants. When less than five hundred feet of water separated them, the Confederate vessel's overstrained engines broke down. She swung sideways and drifted out of action. Whereupon another Confederate ram, the *General Price*, raced in to take her place. *The Monarch*'s sharp beak struck the *General Price* just behind her prow, raked along her side, ripped off a paddle wheel, and chopped a hole in her wooden hull. An eye-witness described the creaking and groaning of the two cumbersome wooden boats as terrible. As the *General Price* sank slowly, Alfred Ellet swung his victorious but staggering *Monarch* around toward the other Confederate rams. Upstream, the rest of Ellet's fleet hurried into the action.

In a deadly way, the scene was reminiscent of a bump-a-car ride at an amusement park, when drivers try to collide with each other in a jumbled mass of confusion.

Not many months earlier, the *General Bragg* had been a civilian ship carrying Southern passengers between ports on the Gulf of Mexico. Now as a ram she undertook to save the day for the Confederacy. Her pilot steered her straight toward the side of the *Monarch*, aiming at the Northerner's paddle wheel. But fate and a sharpshooter on the *Monarch*'s deck decreed otherwise. A bullet from his carbine killed the *General Bragg*'s pilot. Another man

After Memphis surrendered, following the victory of the Union fleet, the city's wharves were crowded with steamboats loading cotton and sugar for shipment up the Mississippi to Northern cities.

jumped into the fallen steersman's place. He too was shot down. With no one at its wheel, the Confederate boat continued to steam toward the *Monarch*, but in an erratic manner.

From the other side, the *Beauregard* also pointed her nose at the *Monarch* and charged. Again, luck helped the North. Taking advantage of the *Monarch*'s superior speed, her pilot skillfully swung the boat so that both Confederate vessels missed her. Instead, they smashed into each other and both sank.

In less than an hour, the Battle of the Rams was over, with overwhelming victory for the North. The remaining Confederate boats were sunk or captured by the Northern gunboats. Broken hulls of sunken boats cluttered the river channel and debris littered the shores. Memphis had no defenses other than the vanquished fleet. Triumphantly, Ellet sent one of his sons, who had sailed with him, ashore to raise the Stars and Stripes above the city's post office. Not only had Ellet led a major victory for the North but also he had shown those reluctant Northern admirals who had scorned him that ordinary riverboats made fine amateur warships.

CHAPTER NINE

Sailing the Great Lakes

WHILE steamboats carried one throng of settlers and adventurers along the Ohio and Mississippi rivers, another procession migrated westward along a second great water route farther to the north, the Great Lakes. Those who reached Buffalo, New York, by way of the Erie Canal were in most instances still far from their chosen destinations on the frontier. From Buffalo, they faced another journey by water into the heart of the country. This time they rode aboard the sailing ships and steamships that sailed their way to the West along the often stormy waters of the Great Lakes.

Sometimes called the Five Sisters, the Great Lakes hang like a bunch of grapes suspended from the border between the United States and Canada. Together, the five lakes—inland seas, really— are so big that if the fresh water of the Great Lakes were spread evenly over the old forty-eight states, the United States would be flooded to a depth of ten feet.

Buffalo lies at the northeastern tip of Lake Erie. Just north of it, water from Erie tumbles over the majestic heights of Niagara Falls into Lake Ontario and then eastward through the St. Lawrence River into the Atlantic Ocean. Our concern is primarily with the four lakes to the west of Buffalo—Lake Erie, Lake Huron, Lake Michigan, and Lake Superior

A ship leaving Buffalo goes west through Lake Erie, northwest

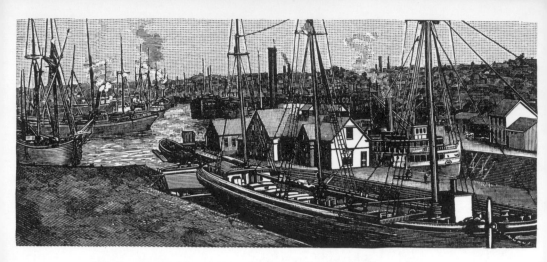

Dock scene at Cleveland, an important Great Lakes port

through Lake Huron to the Straits of Mackinac, then either south down the length of Lake Michigan to Chicago or west through the "Soo" Canal at Sault Ste. Marie into mighty Lake Superior. At the farthest end of Lake Superior the vessel docks at the twin ports of Duluth, Minnesota, and Superior, Wisconsin—just twelve less than a thousand miles from the departure wharf at Buffalo.

Nature created two major barriers to travel on the Great Lakes, but human ingenuity overcame both of them. The Welland Canal was built around Niagara Falls, so ships could move by a series of locks from Lake Ontario to the higher altitude of Lake Erie. At Sault Ste. Marie, the rocky, swiftly falling St. Mary's River was an impossible bottleneck that kept ships from entering Lake Superior until construction of the Soo Locks.

Uncounted thousands of immigrants from Europe, along with Americans from the eastern states whose itchy feet caused them to follow the frontier, sailed the Great Lakes to their new homes during the 1800s. With them they carried piles of household goods, trunks filled with cherished possessions from the homes they had left across the ocean, and bright hopes for the future.

There was, as a typical example, a thin, sandy-haired Scottish lad named John Muir. When he was eleven, in 1849, his father decided to leave the family home in Scotland and move to North America, probably somewhere in Canada. The father couldn't afford to take along his wife and all eight of their children, so he had the adventurous voyage with three of them, John and a brother and sister. The mother and the other children would come later. First the father must establish their new home and save up enough money.

The Muirs had a dreary crossing of the Atlantic on a sailing ship that lasted six and a half weeks. They followed the immigrant procession by boat up the Hudson River from New York City, then journeyed slowly along the Erie Canal to Buffalo. Mr. Muir was a stern man, much given to quoting from the Bible, and a determined one, but he had crossed the ocean without a specific destination in mind. He was still uncertain when they reached Buffalo. But on the docks of the Great Lakes boats, he saw a schooner unloading a cargo of splendid-looking wheat.

"Where does that grain come from?" he asked a grain merchant standing nearby.

"It was grown in Wisconsin." The merchant said the boat had taken it aboard at Milwaukee.

The look of such a fine crop was enough for Mr. Muir. He decided that the family would settle in Wisconsin and booked passage on a steamer to Milwaukee. Aboard with them, the Muirs had boxes of farm equipment and provisions for setting up a homestead, including carpentering tools, a scythe, and an iron stove.

John's blue eyes sparkled at the sights of the New World as the

Old map shows many steamer routes on the Great Lakes.

steamship chuffed its way the length of Lake Erie and up the narrows past the little town of Detroit. At the Straits of Mackinac he saw Indians and bark wigwams. When the boat sailed down Lake Michigan, it was like being out on the ocean again—heavy choppy waves that made the vessel roll, and no land to be seen in any direction.

After the Muirs came ashore at Milwaukee, Mr. Muir hired a farmer to haul them and their goods by wagon over a muddy trail a hundred miles into the countryside. There they built a farm of their own.

The story of the Muirs is representative of the many thousand families who followed the Great Lakes route toward the West. Young Johnny became so fascinated with the natural beauty of the broad American continent that he devoted his life to protecting it. We know him as the famous naturalist, John Muir.

The first boat to venture onto the Great Lakes above Niagara Falls was built and sailed by the French explorer Robert Cavelier, Sieur de la Salle. In 1679, the *Griffin* spread her sails and headed west from the Buffalo area, where she had been constructed from timbers hewn out of the forest. She was sixty feet long, tiny by our standards but huge when compared to the canoes the Indians paddled along the shores. La Salle's plan was to go into Lake Michigan, buy furs from the Indians, and ship them back to Montreal.

Not only was the *Griffin* the first boat to sail the Great Lakes but also it was the first to vanish without a trace, a fate that was to befall many Lake boats in coming centuries.

At Green Bay on the western shore of Lake Michigan, La Salle supervised the loading of the *Griffin* with stacks of fur pelts. While the boat carried them back east, La Salle and a party of men were to explore down Lake Michigan to the south. With a farewell salute from her single cannon, the *Griffin* sailed away, never to be heard from again. Probably she sank in a storm with all hands lost.

Walk-in-the-Water was the strange name of the first steamboat

*Representation of Robert Cavelier,
Sieur de la Salle, at the mouth of the
Mississippi*

on the Great Lakes, recalling the way an astonished Indian described the first trip of Robert Fulton's *Clermont* up the Hudson. She sailed from Buffalo in 1818, using sails to reinforce the low power of her steam engine and side paddle wheels. For three years, little *Walk-in-the-Water* puffed and splashed her way around Lake Erie with passengers and freight, until she was blown ashore near Buffalo in a gale. Her crew was able to tie her to a tree, so everyone aboard got ashore safely before the boat sank. That was in 1821, at a time when steamboats were becoming numerous on the Ohio and Mississippi rivers.

Thus steamboat traffic on the Great Lakes was established before the Erie Canal opened in 1825, and vessels were ready to carry the immigrants west from Buffalo.

Since the Great Lakes are deep, the vessels that sail on them always have been designed more like ocean-going ships than the flat-bottomed, wedding-cake style steamboats of the rivers. Raging storms swirl across the Lakes, during the late fall and winter months, especially in November. Ice-laden winds that have gathered momentum across hundreds of miles of the Canadian Arctic swoop down out of the north, creating high-breaking waves that test the strength of the finest ships. Waves on the Great Lakes are shorter and choppier than the long swells of the Atlantic Ocean; this increases the danger that a ship caught in a severe storm may break in half.

Because vessels on the Great Lakes are always relatively close to land, compared to the hundreds of miles of open water in the Atlantic, it might seem that sailing on the Lakes would be much safer than on the Atlantic. This isn't true. Starting with the *Griffin* three hundred years ago, approximately six thousand ships of substantial size have been sunk on the Great Lakes. The bottoms of the lakes are littered with wreckage. In Green Bay, the long western arm of Lake Michigan that extends behind the Door Peninsula of Wisconsin, diving with snorkels, wetsuits, and air tanks to inspect sunken wrecks is a popular recreation. Wreckage of more than two hundred boats has been charted on the bottom in that area alone. Even the remains of the *Griffin* may lie there, waiting to be found by some fortunate diver.

While hundreds of thousands of persons made safe, uneventful voyages on the lakes during the 147 years that passenger vessels operated, the roll of victims of shipwrecks, fires, and mysterious disappearances is enormous. In the notorious storm of November, 1913, more than thirty boats either sank or were wrecked when driven onto the rocks. Sailing on the Great Lakes can be treacherous because of unexpected changes in wind direction, precipitous drops in temperature, and the heavy coating of ice that often encases vessels in winter. Because of ice and snow, shipping on the Great Lakes ceases for several months each year. Vessels frequently become icebound when their captains try to squeeze in one trip too many as winter descends.

Fascinating tales of Great Lakes shipwrecks are spun when seamen gather on a winter night. One is about the passenger steamer *Lady Elgin* and the lumber schooner *Augusta* that sent her to the bottom of Lake Michigan one night. The year was 1860, a few weeks before the election in which Abraham Lincoln was chosen President. A group of Irishmen in Milwaukee who supported his opponent, Stephen A. Douglas, chartered the *Lady Elgin*, the finest craft in Milwaukee, for excursion to Chicago, where Douglas was to hold a campaign rally. Calling themselves the Union Guard, the Irish men and women had a gala hundred-mile voyage down to Chicago, hollered themselves hoarse for Douglas at the meeting, and were holding a lively dance aboard the *Lady Elgin* homeward bound late at night. Fog had settled over Lake Michigan. As the *Lady Elgin* sailed along ten miles offshore, opposite the northern Chicago suburb of Winnetka, she was struck hard amidships by the *Augusta*. Neither ship had seen the other. In the 1800s, vessels had neither radio nor radar to guide them.

For a few minutes the bow of the *Augusta* was stuck deep in the *Lady Elgin*'s side; then the wooden schooner pulled free. Through a megaphone, a voice in the dark called to the passenger boat, "Shall I stand by? Will you need help, Captain?"

The *Lady Elgin*'s captain replied proudly that his steamer could take care of herself and that the *Augusta* should try to make port. So the old sailing ship struggled safely to Chicago. Not so the *Lady Elgin*. The blow in her side was fatal. A few minutes after the schooner disappeared in the fog, the passenger vessel sank, so suddenly that none of her lifeboats was launched. Everyone aboard drowned, all three hundred of them. Within minutes, the happy, laughing Irish party had turned into tragedy.

Bitterness in Milwaukee against the *Augusta* was so intense that her owners changed her name and painted her black. But the next year when the schooner, now called the *Colonel Cook*, was loading

Great Lakes steamer leaves Milwaukee, as did the ill-fated Lady Elgin.

in Milwaukee, the Irish learned of her presence and made plans to burn her that night in revenge. Tipped off to the plot, her captain sailed the schooner out of the harbor just in time. He took the vessel through the Great Lakes, down the St. Lawrence River, and out into the Atlantic Ocean. In New York, she was sold to new owners. Not until years later, when tempers had cooled, did the lumber schooner return to Lake Michigan.

At least, the exact cause of that wreck was known. This wasn't the case twenty years later, also in Lake Michigan, with the sturdy side-wheeler *Alpena*.

In the years before automobiles and good highways, travel by horse-drawn vehicles was slow, and trips by train between small cities often required long delays when passengers had to change from one train to another. Trips by Lake steamer, often involving overnight rides, were more pleasant. Scheduled passenger service was a popular way to travel. That was the *Alpena*'s role, carrying passengers and light freight between the ports of western Michigan and Chicago.

She sailed from Grand Haven, Michigan, about nine o'clock on the night of Friday, October 15, 1880, with about sixty passengers on the overnight trip southwest across Lake Michigan to Chicago. Everything was normal as she steamed out through the Grand

Haven breakwater into choppy seas. Those on shore watched her lights dwindle in the distance.

Early on Saturday morning, a great storm arose. Snow swirled around, and the temperature nose-dived into the thirties. The *Alpena* didn't arrive at her Chicago dock as scheduled on Saturday morning, but no one was surprised. Many other vessels had been delayed and limped into port hours late. Concern grew when the *Alpena* didn't arrive on Sunday, either. Or on Monday. Obviously something had happened.

What made the disappearance of the *Alpena* so strange was that four other boats reported seeing her at various places on Lake Michigan during Saturday. Once she was only thirty-five miles from Chicago. Another time she was sighted off Kenosha, Wisconsin, apparently headed for land; a third time, off Racine, Wisconsin, headed back into the middle of the lake. Never did she signal to other vessels that she was in trouble, or wanted help.

In the middle of the following week, pieces of wreckage from the *Alpena* floated to shore—not on the western side of Lake Michigan, where it might be expected, but on the eastern, or Michigan, side near where she had started her voyage on Friday night. Among the debris were the piano from her lounge, a portion of her oval staircase, and parts of the printing on the casing of a paddle wheel. Also, seven empty pine coffins, part of the cargo she had been carrying. All four of her lifeboats drifted to land empty, and twenty-five unused life preservers found their way ashore.

Among the passengers were a minister from Chicago and his nineteen-year-old bride from a little Michigan town. They had been married at her home on Friday and were sailing to Chicago on their honeymoon. The bride's father walked up and down the shore for days, hoping to recover their bodies. All he found was their trunk, cast up on the beach.

Few bodies from the *Alpena* were ever found. In the clothing on two of them, searchers found pocket watches that had stopped at 10:55. But 10:55 A.M. or P.M., of what day? Saturday night, Sunday, or even Monday morning? Nobody ever found out. A hundred years later, the mystery of the wandering *Alpena* and why she sank, and where, remains unsolved, probably forever.

Sharing the lakes with the passenger boats were freighters that in later years grew to enormous size. They hauled bulk cargoes of iron ore, grain, lumber, coal, and limestone, and still do. These ships are of a special design for lake use, differing from the shape of most ocean vessels but somewhat resembling the supertankers that carry oil across the oceans. Their cabins and equipment are at the stern, with only a small deckhouse at the bow. In between are cargo holds hundreds of feet in length.

Ocean-going cargo ships have been sailing up the St. Lawrence River into the Great Lakes for many decades. Lakes seamen call them "salties" because their normal home is in the salt water. Since the long, broad St. Lawrence Seaway locks were built in 1959, freighters flying the flags of many nations are a common sight on the lakes. Before the Seaway, only relatively small freighters could pass through the old locks around the rapids of the St. Lawrence. Their captains had to check their cargo weight closely, in order to get the ships through. The captain of a Norwegian freighter loading at Cleveland one time discovered that his cargo lowered the ship too deep into the water. He lightened the ship just enough by leaving the spare anchor behind on the dock. Afterward, he wondered if the local children had enjoyed climbing on the "plaything" he had left them.

Although they never were adorned with as much "gingerbread" as the Mississippi River steamboats, Great Lakes passenger ships in later years offered fine accommodations. They were much sturdier than the riverboats, being built of steel in later years and often using propellers like ocean vessels, rather than paddle wheels.

After the Canadian and American railroads were built across the continent, combined lake-and-railroad trips became popular. A brochure published by a tour company in 1910 advertised a six-week trip that provided a spectacular view of North America. The tour group sailed the Great Lakes from Buffalo to Duluth, traveled across western Canada on a Canadian Pacific train through the

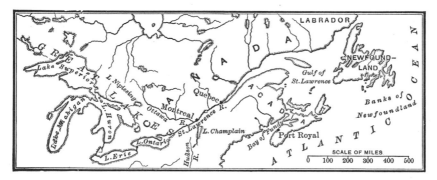

The Great Lakes and the St. Lawrence River

Rocky Mountains to Seattle, and from there sailed aboard an ocean steamer up the inland passage along the Pacific Coast to Alaska. After returning to Seattle, they rode east by train to Yellowstone National Park and from there back to Duluth; there they boarded the Great Lakes steamer *Northwest* for the return ride to Buffalo. Describing the Lakes steamer, the advertising said: "In finishing and furnishing, the *Northwest* is the equal of the finest ocean steamship ever built."

The tour promoters made a special appeal to women traveling alone, or with another woman, such as two widows together. Today such traveling arrangements are commonplace; in 1900 they were relatively rare. The company reassured the women thus: "Ladies Without Escort can make the trip without experiencing the slightest unpleasantness or being in any way oppressed by the doubts and difficulties incident to travel in the ordinary way."

Just as the *J. M. White III* was the biggest and finest of the Mississippi River packets, the *Seeandbee* was widely regarded as about the finest of the Great Lakes vessels, although the *Greater Detroit* and her sister ship, the *Greater Buffalo*, were a bit longer. The *Seeandbee* was 500 feet long and nearly 100 feet wide, had six decks and 510 staterooms. Driven by two huge side paddle wheels, she had a cruising speed of 18½ miles an hour. Her grand saloon, or main public cabin, rose three stories high and was elaborately furnished. For years the *Seeandbee* made overnight voyages

123

between Cleveland and Buffalo. (Her name came from the Cleveland and Buffalo Transit Company.)

By the time of World War II in the early 1940s, passenger travel on the Great Lakes declined because people drove, flew, or went by train instead. But the *Seeandbee* had a valuable and exciting second life before finally going onto the scrap heap. Her upper decks were stripped away, a 550-foot flight deck was welded in their place, and she became the aircraft carrier *U.S.S. Wolverine*. A side-wheeler aircraft carrier! Altogether, eighteen thousand student Navy aviators learned how to make landings on her deck as she sailed around Lake Michigan.

Of the hundreds of passenger ships that once sailed the Great Lakes, only one is still afloat, and she hasn't sailed under her own power for some twenty years. She is the *Keewatin*, built in Scotland in 1908, in the same shipyard at the same time as the doomed ocean liner, the *Lusitania*. For fifty-seven years, the *Keewatin* and her sister ship, the *Assiniboia*, sailed between Georgian Bay, an eastern arm of Lake Huron, and the northwestern end of Lake Superior. They had the distinction of being the last two passenger ships operating on the Great Lakes, at the time they were taken out of service in November, 1965. Later the *Assiniboia* burned. The *Keewatin* is docked at Douglas, Michigan, on the eastern shore of Lake Michigan, and during the summer is open for tours. Everything aboard is as it was during her sailing days; the dining room tables are set with linen and silver, ready to serve passengers who will never come aboard again. A visitor to the *Keewatin* gets a fine sense of what passenger travel on the Great Lakes was like.

The gigantic ore boats sailing the Great Lakes today have intricate safety devices, including radio-telephone service to shore and to other ships, radar, and sonar. The vessels are built with engineering wisdom accumulated for hundreds of years. Yet not long ago the treacherous waters claimed one of these huge vessels, almost from under the noses of other ships close by.

She was the *Edmund Fitzgerald*, whose tragic fate has been remembered by folk singers in a popular ballad. The *"Fitz"* was very

With black smoke pouring from her stack, the S.S. Keewatin *loads passengers at Owen Sound for a one-day excursion trip on Georgian Bay. The photograph was taken about 1934.*

large, 729 feet long and 75 feet wide, and had holds so spacious that she carried 25,000 tons of cargo.

It was sunny and relatively warm when the *Edmund Fitzgerald* sailed from Superior, Wisconsin, on November 9, 1975, with a load of taconite pellets, bound for Detroit. But November is a perilous month on the Great Lakes. Storms often sweep down suddenly from Canada. That is precisely what happened as the *Fitzgerald*, low in the water, plowed eastward through Lake Superior toward the locks at Sault Ste. Marie. Enormous waves smashed against her, snow and ice accumulated on her deck. But she was built for such weather and had gone through severe storms many times before.

As the *Fitz* moved along, Captain Ernest McSorley talked by radio telephone several times with the captain of another ore boat, the *Arthur M. Anderson*, sailing along the same route a short dis-

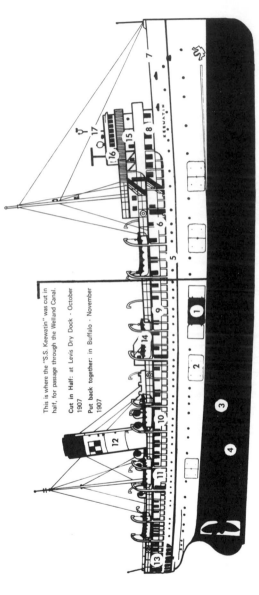

This is where the "S.S. Keewatin" was cut in half, for passage through the Welland Canal.

Cut in Half: at Lewis Dry Dock - October 1907

Put back together: in Buffalo - November 1907

1. **Entrance:** Information Booth, Tour Ticket Sales, Coffee Shop, and "The Cargo Deck". Gift Shop. (the cargo deck was renovated to create this present site.)

2. **Lobby:** the passengers of the Keewatin entered here. The Pursers Office and Barber Shop are located in this area.

3. **Boiler Room:** Here is where the "firemen" hand-stoked the fireholds 24 hours a day in four hour shifts.

4. **Engine Room:** The quadruple expansion steam engine produced 3,300 horsepower giving this "queen of the Lakes" a cruising speed of 14 knots. (high pressure cylinder: 27" bore — low pressure cylinder: 76" bore.)

5. **Staterooms:** There are 108 rooms on two passenger decks (all had running water). The comfortable but limited second-class and third-class accommodations are contrasted with the "luxurious" first-class suites.

6. **Promenade Deck:** Where the passengers strolled in fair weather.

7. **Bow:** Off-limits to all former passengers — features include the anchor chain, anchor windlasses and docking gear.

8. **Forward lounge:** This room was designed and furnished for the ladies, where they could get together for tea or a game of cards.

9. **Flower Well:** A room two-decks high with an open "airy" feeling due to the stainglassed skylight and pots of plants. It was here the passengers were served bouillon at 10:00 a.m. and tea at 4:00 p.m.

10. **Dining Room:** Seats 120 - Passengers entered into the Edwardian elegance of the saloon with mahogany paneling and polished brass.

11. **Galley:** Here is where the Chinese cooks prepared over 1,000 meals a day on the fourteen foot cast-iron coal stove.

12. **Funnel:** Painted as it was when the Keewatin was in service. It proudly displays the C.P.R. House flag.

13. **Ballroom and Observation Deck:** The hand-carved panels in this room depict the different nationalities of the territories ruled by Great Britain in the 1900's. (also used as a cinema)

14. **Lifeboats:** The Keewatin carries 10.

15. **Captain's Suite:** High in the ship's superstructure was the shipboard home of the Captain. (It is preserved just as it was left by the last Captain)

16. **Bridge:** was normally manned by a complement of four: the watch officer, navigating officer, quarter master and helmsmen.

17. **Top of the Wheel House:** The Keewatin's upmost deck is the location of the Radar, Direction Finder and Radio Antenna.

A side-view drawing of the S.S. Keewatin, showing location of her various features. The "Kee" was a typical twentieth-century Great Lakes passenger ship.

tance behind. The *Anderson* could see the *Fitz* on her radar screen. McSorley commented that his ship had developed a list but didn't seem especially worried about it.

In early evening, McSorley told the *Anderson*, "We are going along like an old shoe. No problems at all."

A few minutes later, the *Edmund Fitzgerald* disappeared from the *Anderson*'s radar, nor could she be reached by radio telephone. The *Anderson* alerted other ships in the area. The massive vessel had vanished, suddenly and without warning, carrying her crew of twenty-nine to the bottom with her. Eventually the ship was located by sonar, lying on the bottom 530 feet below the surface, broken in half. By use of an ingenious machine, underwater pictures were taken of the wreckage. There is no proof that the *Edmund Fitzgerald* broke in two on the surface; many experts believe that she did not and that the break came when she hit bottom. But why did she sink? Despite an elaborate investigation, no one is sure of anything, except that once more the Great Lakes had seized a victim, the largest and most modern one yet.

No longer do the Great Lakes carry travelers toward the West. Neither do the Mississippi River and its main tributaries, the Ohio and Missouri rivers. But back in the 1800s, when they did so in great numbers, they formed a water route of enormous length for anyone who chose to use it, all the way from New York City to the Rocky Mountains of western Montana. A traveler could go across New York State via the Erie Canal, by steamboat from Buffalo to Ohio, down the length of that state by canalboat to the Ohio River, from Cincinnati to St. Louis, Missouri, aboard a steamboat, and from St. Louis aboard a smaller steamboat far up the Missouri River to Fort Benton, Montana. The total distance was approximately 4100 miles. Probably few if any inquisitive travelers ever sailed the entire length of this slow and twisting water route, but it could be done. The most adventurous, frustrating, and unpredictable portion of the journey was up the Missouri River.

CHAPTER TEN

Steamboats vs. Indians

ALTHOUGH the Missouri River is a tributary of the Mississippi River, it has a personality all its own. From its source in the Rocky Mountains of Montana, the Big Muddy twists and turns for nearly three thousand miles in a generally eastward course, with meanderings north and south, until its grimy waters pour into the Mississippi River just above St. Louis. It flows through canyons and across hundreds of miles of prairie, its bed pockmarked with rapids and shallows, its surface ripped by dust storms and tornadoes. During the middle and late 1800s, the Missouri was a great water highway to the West, along which settlers, soldiers, and gold hunters migrated.

That word "highway" must be used cautiously. The Missouri might properly be called a watery interstate superhighway in its lower reaches, across the state of Missouri from its mouth to Kansas City and a bit beyond. After that it diminishes into something like a two-lane highway, and by the time the traveler gets upstream across the Dakotas into Montana, the Missouri has dwindled into a one-lane country road that can't quite decide where it wants to go. A traveler before the Civil War described the river as "unpoetic and repulsive—a stream of flowing mud studded with dead tree trunks and broken by bars."

Yet steamboats driven by stubborn captains struggled up the

Typical of the rugged, shallow-draft steamboats that plied the upper portion of the Missouri River after the Civil War, the heavily laden Rosebud *pushes ahead with clouds of black smoke coming from her stacks.*

Winter brought special dangers to steamboats. The Georgia Lee *and* De Soto *were wrecked by floating ice on the Mississippi River and went aground on the rocks.*

treacherous river all the way to Fort Benton, Montana, 2600 miles above St. Louis. The boats went aground almost endlessly, were flipped over by high winds, had their bottoms ripped out by sunken trees and ice slabs, were engulfed by swarms of mosquitoes, and fought running gun battles with Indians. This was no place for the elegant floating palaces that plied the Mississippi. Missouri River steamboats were smaller, tougher, and plainer, real frontier types, so flat bottomed that those on the upper river drew only thirty inches of water. Usually they were stern-wheelers, which are better than side-wheelers in shallow water.

As the decades passed, steamboating on the lower Missouri came to resemble the Mississippi River trade, on a lesser scale, with scheduled service and fairly large boats in operation. But on the remote upper stretches of the river, the smaller "mountain" boats that looked like ragged country cousins were the ones that got through.

Once when a large lower-river boat, the *Imperial*, made an experimental trip far upriver, on her return voyage she became stuck on 132 separate sandbars and finally became so battered that she had to be abandoned a thousand miles above St. Louis.

Another curse of the Missouri was the mud. Water drawn from the river to make steam was so full of silt that it clogged the boilers. When a Missouri boat stopped for the night—few of them dared to travel after dark—her fires were extinguished and a roustabout climbed into the boilers to shovel out the steaming mud.

Nobody could be sure for long which way the Missouri would flow during the 1800s. It changed course constantly, as its waters cut new channels and abandoned old ones, even more casually than those of the Mississippi did. A settlement built on the Missouri's banks might find itself high and dry a few months later, as the fickle current dug a new channel a mile or so away in the sandy soil. The Sioux City, Iowa, *Register*, a newspaper published in a town along the river's banks, once commented, "Of all the variable things in creation the most uncertain are the action of a jury, the state of a woman's mind, and the condition of the Missouri River."

For example, a farmer in 1896 dug a well on his property several miles from the Missouri River. To his surprise, several feet down in the hole he found a Bible with the name *Naomi* on its cover. He sent the Bible to Captain Joseph La Barge, a famous steamboat captain, in search of clues as to how it happened to be in such a peculiar place. Captain La Barge had the answer. Fifty-six years earlier, the steamboat *Naomi* had been wrecked on the Missouri at the precise place where the farmer was digging his well. In those times, missionaries frequently left Bibles on the steamboats for use by passengers, chained down so no one could walk off with them. Usually the name of the boat was printed on the Bible's cover. The *Naomi's* wreckage had been buried under the silt, farmland had been built up by the flowing mud, and crops grew where the river once flowed. In the intervening half century, the stream bed had shifted several miles away.

Steamboat captains during the 1800s had enough trouble finding a passable channel without wondering where the channel would be fifty years later.

Missouri River steamboating was restricted to a few months in spring, summer, and early fall. The rest of the year the river was either too low or frozen over. Captains who tried to stretch the season frequently found their boats stuck in the ice for the winter at a remote place.

Often a boat trapped on a sandbar was set free by a slow, laborious self-rescue maneuver called "grasshoppering." Each mountain steamboat carried two long, heavy spars that resembled telephone poles near the bow. When a boat became stuck and couldn't work free after the passengers and the freight had been taken off, the crew jammed one end of each pole into the sandbar. The tops were high in the air, angled slightly. Heavy ropes were strung from the forward deck up to the top of each spar through a block and tackle, and back down to a revolving capstan on the deck. Husky crewmen turned the capstan, reeling in the ropes. At the same time, the paddle wheel was turned, to provide forward power. The result was like taking a step with a pair of crutches. The boat dragged itself forward a few feet. Time after time the noisy process was repeated, until the vessel pulled itself across the sandbar. This might require an entire day, or even two. The name grasshoppering was given to this awkward procedure because the long spars and attached lines looked like the front legs of those insects, and the boat went forward in little hops.

Hardly anyone except roving bands of Indians lived in the thousands of square miles of plains and mountains along the Missouri's course when the first steamboat, the *Independence*, pushed its way about two hundred miles above St. Louis in 1819. That same year the Indians along the banks were astonished to see a creature that looked like a huge monster coming up the river, puffing steam from its nostrils. Its sides were painted with black scales. This was the *Western Engineer*, the result of a designer's wild idea. He thought that if he shaped the steamboat to look like a sea serpent, and piped the exhaust steam forward out of its snout, the Indians would be frightened and stay away from it.

The Indians did leave the *Western Engineer* alone, not because they were frightened by this weird "fire canoe" but because in those days they had not yet built up enough anger against the white man and his trickery to attack his boats. That came later.

At first, the Missouri River was used only by fur traders to bring their pelts down from the Montana and Dakota territories in keelboats, and flatboats with oars called Mackinaws. Later the Army built small forts at widely scattered points along the river. Since these few forts and fur-trading posts were the only habitation, steamboats had scant reason to struggle up the Missouri except on occasional supply trips; they carried fur shipments on their return voyages. The soldiers who manned the forts traveled to their posts by steamboat.

Traffic increased after the discovery of gold in California started the Forty-Niners on their long trek west. Immigrants and would-be gold miners came up the Missouri on steamboats to the mouth of the Platte River, near Omaha. From there they traveled west overland along the Oregon Trail up the Platte valley. Mormons going to their church's new home at Salt Lake City, Utah, also rode the steamboats up the Missouri, to make the overland trip as short as possible.

Watching buffalo roam on the prairie was a diversion for passengers on the tedious voyages. When the huge, shaggy animals stood near the riverbank or ventured into the water, passengers shot at them, sometimes killing one for fresh meat on the boat. When the *Ida Stockdale* one day approached an open space called Elk Horn Meadow, because elk came there in the spring to shed their horns, those aboard saw an astonishing sight. Thousands of buffalo in a massive herd rumbled up to the riverbank and plunged in. Bellowing and pawing as they swam across, they formed a black mass in the water so thick that the boat could not move. Buffalo bumped against the sides of the vessel. Some became entangled in the blades of the stern wheel. Reaching the other bank, they thundered off across the prairie in billowing dust. The *Ida*

The Benton, *a veteran of the mountainous upper reaches of the Missouri River, lies in its final resting place near Sioux City after hitting a bridge and drifting ashore with a broken back.*

Stockdale was forced to wait for several hours until the river was clear enough for her to break through the floundering stragglers.

During the Civil War, in 1862, gold was discovered in Montana, not far from the source of the Missouri. That brought a rush of passengers on the steamboats and inspired captains to push their vessels farther and farther upstream, despite the immense difficulties involved. Finally, the ragged group of log buildings called Fort Benton, Montana, became the head of navigation, the farthest settlement a steamboat could reach. If a captain happened to be lucky, and the Missouri was high enough from spring rains and mountain snow runoff, he might maneuver his boat from St. Louis to Fort Benton in nine or ten weeks.

The Indians, particularly the Sioux and the Blackfeet, had roamed these hunting grounds for hundreds of years. They watched with growing anger as the numbers of white settlers increased. When the Indians signed treaties with the United States government far away in Washington, D.C., and then saw agents of the government break promises and cheat them out of merchandise they were entitled to receive under the treaties, they began hostilities against the white man. Since the steamboats on the Missouri carried the civilization they feared and didn't understand, the Indians frequently used them as targets for their arrows and gunfire.

When Joseph Marie La Barge was sixteen, he went into the wilds of the upper Missouri River country from St. Louis as a fur trader for the American Fur Company. That was in 1832. A muscular, handsome youth of French-Canadian ancestry, he quickly learned the lore of the Western wilderness and the ways of the huge buffalo herds that roamed the Plains. He traded and mingled with the Indians, who came to respect him for his courage and honesty. He was a hard and daring man—he had to be to survive—but a fair one. Soon he became a clerk, an apprentice pilot, and within a few years a captain on the early Missouri River steamboats. Along the Missouri, it was quite common for a boat's captain to be its pilot as well. For half a century Captain La Barge was a familiar figure along the Big Muddy, and in his later years a legendary one. Although he owned and piloted many boats, he never had one wrecked: a remarkable record.

Captain La Barge took a newly built boat, the *Martha*, up the Missouri in the spring of 1847, carrying a cargo of annuities for distribution to the Indians. These annuities were allotments of cloth, food, and beads that the federal government gave to the Indians under the terms of its peace treaties with the various tribes. This load of goods was assigned to the Sioux, and a government Indian agent was aboard to make the distribution.

When the *Martha* tied up ashore at a trading post downstream from what later became Pierre, South Dakota, the Indian agent gave a feast for the Sioux who gathered there, then delivered the annuities to them. However, he withheld about one-third of the

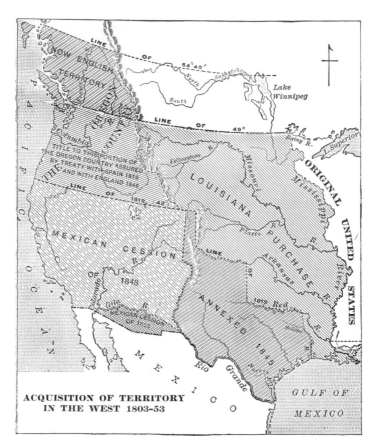

Old map of the West shows the course of the Missouri River.

goods. He told the Indians that they must go up to the fur-trading company's post at Pierre to collect the rest of their annuities.

With reason, the Indians believed that they were being cheated. Sullenly they gathered along the shore, in vain demanding the remaining goods. La Barge explained to them that he could do nothing, as the Indian agent controlled the distribution.

Collecting wood along the barren shores of the Missouri to keep the steamboat fires fed was always difficult. Woodcutting was a dangerous occupation, because Indians frequently shot at anyone who worked around the wood landings.

Captain La Barge had purchased ten cords of firewood at the landing where the *Martha* met the Sioux. He thought he had better take it aboard immediately, because if he left the wood until his return trip the Indians might burn it in revenge. So he ordered crewmen ashore to bring the logs aboard. Each man took a load in his arms, and several were struggling up the gangplank with their burdens. Suddenly the Indians attacked them with rawhide whips. The men were forced to drop their loads into the water and in some cases fell overboard themselves, from the stinging force of the whips. Later, led by a famous mountain man, Etienne Provost, who was a passenger aboard the *Martha*, the battered crewmen made a second dash ashore and loaded the wood safely.

The wind was whipping across the open ground so furiously that La Barge decided to keep the *Martha* tied to shore a while. That, it proved, was a mistake.

The Indians had ridden away, still angry. An hour or so later, when all was quiet, La Barge went to his cabin. His wife, the first white woman to travel into upper Missouri River country, was in her stateroom. A volley of gunfire from shore shattered the silence. Glass on the boat crashed and woodwork splintered from the bullets. La Barge ran to his wife's stateroom, told her to stay inside, and had two men barricade the door with mattresses. Then he heard wild yelling. Emerging from a hiding place, dozens of Indians swarmed up the gangplank and seized control of the front portion of the *Martha*. They poured buckets of water onto the boiler fires, effectively destroying the boat's power.

From the attackers came the demand, "Surrender the boat to us, or we will kill everyone aboard!"

Faced with this crisis, the captain showed the daring and re-sourcefulness that made him famous. While another officer argued with the Indians up front, La Barge and the engineer slipped to the stern of the boat. They lifted a light cannon by a pulley from the main deck to the cabin deck and aimed it at the Indians. La Barge loaded the gun with powder and boiler rivets.

Only a few feet of deck space separated the Indians from La

Passengers go ashore from a Missouri River steamboat under armed guard to inspect the countryside during the late 1800s. The long, slow voyages became boring for the passengers, who had little to entertain them.

Barge and the gun. The captain lit a cigar and held up the smoking tip for the Indians to see, motioning with it toward the fuse of the cannon.

He shouted to the negotiator, "Tell them to get off the boat or I will blow them all to the devil!"

Then, as he told the story later, "At the same time I started for the gun with the lighted cigar in my hand. The effect was complete and instantaneous. The Indians turned and fled and fairly fell over each other in their panic to get off the boat."

A far more deadly confrontation between Captain La Barge and the Sioux took place several years later, in 1863. By this time, hostility between the Sioux and the white men had become intense, after killings by both sides. Again the trouble happened because an Indian agent tried to cheat the Sioux out of the annuity merchandise due to them.

La Barge was hired by the government to carry goods to the Sioux and the Blackfeet aboard two vessels, the *Robert Campbell*, which he piloted, and the smaller *Shreveport*, captained by his younger brother, John. The *Shreveport* went on ahead. At Pierre, a distribution of annuity goods was made from the *Robert Campbell* to the Two Kettles band of the Sioux by the Indian agent aboard.

Only about two-thirds of the merchandise due to these Sioux was distributed, however. Already in a belligerent mood, the Sioux were furious at this treatment.

"We will get revenge," they told La Barge. "We will follow your boat and attack it whenever we can."

What followed is a remarkable story of hit-and-run warfare. Day after day, for six hundred miles up the Missouri as it meandered across the prairie, the Indians on horseback pursued the *Robert Campbell*. Whenever it stopped for wood or had to sail close to shore, Sioux warriors opened fire on passengers and crew. One time a bullet whizzed through the pilothouse, barely missing the man at the wheel. La Barge had the cargo stacked in barricades around the engines, cabins, and other vulnerable points. Every passenger and crewman who carried a gun had it loaded and ready.

At a point upstream, the *Robert Campbell* met the *Shreveport* and transferred part of the cargo to her. The boats sailed on together, staying as close to mid-river as possible.

From the pilothouse one noon, La Barge was surprised to see a hat floating downstream toward the boats. As it drifted near the *Robert Campbell*, the hat rose above the water and La Barge saw a man standing under it. This was Louis Dauphin, the boats' hunter. He had gone out on the prairie before dawn, hoping to shoot an elk or deer for dinner, and had encountered a large gathering of Indians. To escape, he jumped into the river and swam downstream as inconspicuously as possible.

"You are going to have trouble at the Tobacco Garden," Dauphin warned La Barge. "There are at least fifteen hundred Indians gathered there, and they intend to capture the boat."

The "Tobacco Garden" was the rivermen's nickname for an area where Tobacco Creek flowed into the Missouri. Here the Missouri's navigable channel came within thirty yards or so of a cliff-like bank on the south shore. A sandbar hemmed in the channel on the north side. It was a splendid place for an ambush. When the boats arrived there, the Indians had assembled on the south bank, waiting.

After tying up the boats to the sandbar, La Barge yelled ashore to ask the Indians what they wanted. The rest of their annuities, they shouted back. The Indians asked the captain to send a yawl ashore with the Indian agent, Samuel N. Latta. Latta in turn asked that La Barge put the small boat ashore and bring the Indian leaders out to the *Robert Campbell* for a discussion. Knowing the Indians' tricks, La Barge refused to order his crewmen to take the boat. He would allow it to go ashore only with volunteers. Seven crewmen raised their hands, led by Andy Stinger, the steersman. At first the Indian agent said he would go along, but at the last moment he sent word from his cabin that he had suddenly become ill and couldn't go.

When the rowboat touched shore, it was met by three Indians, one with a rifle and two carrying spears. Stinger motioned for them to come aboard, as he had been instructed to do. Instead of stepping onto the boat peacefully, they leapt in among the seven crewmen, attacking them. Within moments, two crewmen were killed by the spears, and the Indian with the gun shot one crewman to death while wounding another. Stinger escaped by jumping into the water on the offshore side and dragging the yawl away from the bank. The other two crewman fell helplessly onto the bottom of the small boat.

Crewmen and passengers on the *Robert Campbell* and the *Shreveport* had been watching intensely, guns drawn. La Barge's boat had two howitzers on the hurricane deck aimed toward the shore, and the *Shreveport* had one. Many passengers and crewmen stood ready with pistols or rifles.

When those on the steamboats saw what the treachery of the

Steamboats maneuvering along the shallow Western rivers frequently ran aground. Here the Expansion *is stuck on a sandbar in the Yellowstone River.*

Indians had done, they didn't hesitate. Both boats let loose at the Indians with a thundering fusillade of howitzer, rifle, and pistol fire, with deadly effect. Eighteen of the Indians were killed and a large number were wounded. Twenty of their horses were shot dead. The rest of the tribesmen fled. And the flaming animosity between the Sioux and the white men on the northern Plains grew more intense.

CHAPTER ELEVEN

Waiting for Custer

To the cluster of men gathered on the deck of the steamboat *Far West* in remote Montana Territory, the sight was pulse tingling. Amid shouts of goodbye, more than six hundred mounted troopers of the renowned U.S. Seventh Cavalry Regiment rode off briskly from their bivouac beside the steamboat to find and destroy the hostile bands of Sioux that had been terrorizing the frontier. The thumping hooves of their horses raised a trail of dust behind them.

Proudly at the head of the column sat Colonel George Armstrong Custer, the flamboyant Indian fighter whose daring victories and dashing ways had made his name famous to Americans everywhere. Out there in the rugged hills somewhere, a large encampment of the Sioux had gathered, among them such famous leaders as Crazy Horse and Sitting Bull. A crucial battle was brewing, and everyone sensed it.

The date was June 22, 1876, barely a week before the United States was to celebrate its one hundredth birthday.

From the deck of the steamboat that served as headquarters of the expedition, a commander of infantry, whose troops were to follow later, shouted, "Now, Custer, don't be greedy, leave a few Indians for us."

Custer waved gaily and called back, "No, I will not."

With spurs jangling and their blue campaign hats set at a rakish angle, the cavalrymen trotted their horses in a long, narrow procession up the grassy valley of Rosebud Creek. Their company flags snapped in the noonday breeze. The rumble of hoofbeats diminished as the column disappeared around a bend. Last to vanish from view was the mule supply train, burdened with fifteen days of rations for the troopers and extra ammunition.

No one in the column or among those left behind on the *Far West* imagined that the Seventh Cavalry was marching toward one of the most disastrous defeats in American military history; that Custer and the soldiers gathered around him in a desperate hilltop defense would be wiped out to the last man.

The idea of a passenger steamboat serving as headquarters for war against the Indians in a rolling, windswept wilderness hundreds of

The steamboat Far West *tied up along the shore of the Missouri River. Note the wood supply piled on deck. The* Far West *accompanied George Armstrong Custer on his fatal expedition against the Sioux and carried survivors of the battle back to the nearest white settlement.*

miles from the nearest civilian settlement may seem surprising. This was possible primarily because of the piloting skill of a mountain river veteran, Captain Grant Marsh.

A year earlier, the Army had hired Captain Marsh to explore the Yellowstone River with his *Josephine*, to find out how far a steamboat could penetrate into the haunts of the Sioux. As a look at a map will show, the upper Missouri River flows more or less west to east across Montana and North Dakota. Near the border between the two states, the Yellowstone River, a long tributary of the Missouri, enters it from a southwesterly direction after flowing down from the Rocky Mountains. In turn, several small rivers flow northward from the mountains into the Yellowstone. One of these is Rosebud Creek. Parallel to it, farther up the Yellowstone to the west, is the Bighorn River. A branch of the Bighorn is called the Little Bighorn.

Pushing the *Josephine* cautiously over sandbars and against swift spring currents, Marsh sailed her where no steamboat had ever been before, up the Yellowstone well beyond the mouth of the Bighorn to a point 483 miles upstream. The *Josephine* was nearly 2500 miles by water from the mouth of the Missouri, in country where fur traders and explorers had been the only white men to penetrate previously.

An ingenious method was used to measure distance along the meandering, unmapped river. Three men were stationed on the hurricane deck, which was exactly 150 feet long. One man stood at the stern to keep the record, the others at the front end. When the boat started upriver, one of the latter chose an object on shore. He walked toward the stern, keeping abreast of this object. When he reached the stern, still even with the shore marker, he had walked 150 feet and the boat had advanced the same distance. The second man did the same thing, while the first hurried back to the front for his next turn. This makeshift system produced mileage information that was surprisingly accurate.

When the Army planned a major campaign against the hostile Indians in 1876 to subdue them permanently and make the country safe for settlers, naturally it turned again to Captain Marsh. This time he used the *Far West*, smaller than the *Josephine* but still able to carry thirty passengers. His mission was to haul supplies for Custer's cavalry and an infantry force up the Missouri, up the Yellowstone, and then up the Bighorn into waters never reached by a steamboat, until the *Far West* was as close to the anticipated battleground as possible.

As protection against Indian arrows and bullets, Captain Marsh installed boiler plate in semicircular form around the *Far West's* pilothouse, head high with an opening in front, and had sacks of grain and cordwood stacked four feet high around the edges of the lower deck.

The Seventh Cavalry rode westward across country from its home post at Fort Abraham Lincoln, which was situated across the Missouri River from Bismarck, North Dakota, a few days before the *Far West* steamed upriver to the fort. The steamboat caught up with the cavalrymen, and horsemen and boat met at a point on the Yellowstone River. From there they moved side by side upstream to the mouth of Rosebud Creek, where the soldiers made camp and the steamboat tied up to the shore.

On the night of June 21, a council of war was held aboard the *Far West*. Clad in blue flannel shirt, buckskin pants, and high boots, Custer came aboard from his tent pitched a few yards away. General Alfred Terry who was in overall command of the campaign, Custer, and Colonel John Gibbon whose infantry troops were approaching from the west sat for hours under a flickering lamp in the cabin, planning their attack. Scouts had brought them signs that the Sioux were camped a few miles up the Little Bighorn.

At noon the next day, Custer's cavalry rode off to battle. In his kit, the commander carried written orders from General Terry: " . . . proceed up the Rosebud in pursuit of the Indians whose trail was discovered by Major Reno a few days since . . . "

After the cavalry had gone, and the generals had left to join the approaching infantry, Captain Marsh sailed the *Far West* to the mouth of the Bighorn, took her more than fifty miles up that

Cabin of the Far West, *where Custer held a council of war with other Army commanders the night before he led his troops into the battle on the Little Bighorn.*

previously unexplored stream, and tied her up at the point where its tributary, the Little Bighorn, flowed in. The squat *Far West* was a lonely island of civilization in the huge emptyness of the land. Men on her decks could see the smoke of Indian campfires on the southern horizon.

Those on the *Far West* could do little but wait. They felt left out, being so close to the battle that they knew must be going on but having no immediate role in it. To pass the time, Marsh and a few others went fishing in the steamboat's yawl, upstream from the *Far West.*

Without warning, a mounted Indian, clad only in a breech clout and holding his carbine aloft with both hands in a sign of peace, burst through a thicket of willows on the south bank. Startled at first, the fishermen were relieved to see by the erect scalp lock that he was a friendly Crow, not a Sioux. They recognized him as a scout for Custer called Curley. Taking the excited Indian aboard, they rowed back to the *Far West*. Curley spoke no English, and the boatmen knew none of the Crow language. Yet it was clear to them that he was extremely upset. On the deck, Curley groaned and cried, rocking back and forth in grief. When an officer handed him a pencil and piece of paper, and showed him how to use them, Curley sprawled flat on his stomach. He drew a circle, then another outside it. In the space between the circles he stabbed many dots with the pencil point and cried, "*Sioux! Sioux!*"

Inside the smaller circle he made more dots. This time he exclaimed, "*Absaroka! Absaroka!*"

"I know what that means," Captain Marsh said. "It means 'soldiers.' That Englishman, Courtney, who runs the woodyard at the head of Drowned Man's Rapids, told me so."

Curley jumped to his feet, swung his arms wide, and struck his chest repeatedly with his fingers, like bullets. Each time he jabbed himself, he said, "*Poof! Poof! Poof! Absaroka!*" Next he tugged upward at his scalp lock with one hand while making a circle around it with another, and pretended to hang something at his belt while breaking into a Sioux war dance. Scalped!

Captain Baker, an Army man aboard, realized what Curley was trying to tell them. "We're whipped!" he said.

Thus did the first news of Custer's defeat reach those away from the battlefield. When another scout, a white man, reached the boat the next day from the infantry force, which had arrived at the scene after the battle, the full scope of the disaster became known.

Approaching the camp on the Little Bighorn where the Sioux and several other tribes were gathered, Custer had divided his men into groups for the attack. He rode off to the right with 225 of the men. Other columns moved to the left and the center. Obviously Custer had grossly underestimated how many Indians faced his cavalry. His own detachment was outnumbered five to one. Sioux warriors in fantastic war paint, armed with rifles, lances, clubs, and bows and arrows, galloped in from every direction, screaming and shouting. They swarmed around Custer and his detachment on a hill. The cavalrymen used what sparse shelter they could find and

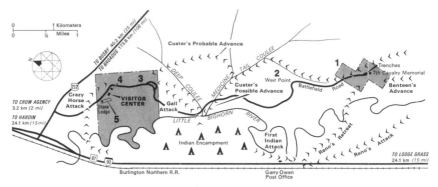

Map of the Little Bighorn battlefield

fought courageously, but within minutes the Indians had killed everyone.

Another column led by Major Marcus A. Reno had been driven back onto a hilltop some distance away. Reinforced by the remainder of the Seventh Cavalry, they dug in and fought off the attackers despite heavy losses, until the Indians withdrew the next day when the infantry approached.

The Seventh Cavalry had been smashed. Altogether, about 275 men were killed and 52 wounded. For more than a hundred years, military students have argued over the tactics of the battle, and whether Custer made a foolhardy attack at the wrong time. No one, however, disputes the dramatic role the *Far West* played in carrying back to civilization the wounded survivors of Reno's detachment, along with the news.

Word reached Captain Marsh that fifty-two wounded men were being brought to the *Far West* from the battlefield by mule on stretchers improvised from the lodgepoles and coverings of the Indian tepees. He sent out crewmen to build fires at intervals through three miles of marshes beyond the boat. At two o'clock in the morning, by the light of the fires on a stormy night, the wounded men were lifted aboard the boat.

While awaiting their arrival, Captain Marsh had crewmen cut great piles of grass along the riverbanks. This was spread eighteen inches deep on the lower deck behind the boilers and covered with tarpaulins to form a huge bed. The *Far West* had become a hospital boat.

The boat carried one other survivor of the battlefield, a sorrel horse named Comanche. The wounded horse had been ridden by Captain Miles Keogh in Custer's fight and somehow survived, although his master was killed. As the only creature to come through alive, Comanche was given a special stall padded with grass on the after deck. For many years thereafter, Comanche, draped in black, saddled but riderless, marched in all Seventh Cavalry parades.

Marsh navigated the *Far West* down to the mouth of the Bighorn, paused there to ferry Gibbon's infantrymen across the river to safety, then started a remarkable journey that became famous in the history of Western rivers. Running through the night despite the perils of snags and shoals, the *Far West* churned down the Yellowstone, into the Missouri, and eastward toward the Seventh Cavalry's home, Fort Abraham Lincoln. The boat covered seven hundred miles in fifty-four hours—"as fast as a railroad train in a narrow, winding stream," a reporter for the St. Paul *Pioneer Press* described it.

Draped in black, with her American flag at half mast, the *Far West* sailed into Bismarck shortly after midnight on July 5. Her whistle blast brought the settlers running to the riverbank to hear the news. Marsh and two Army officers aroused the local newspaper editor and a telegrapher. The editor immediately wrote a news bulletin addressed to the New York *Herald*, and the telegrapher tapped out the message by dot-and-dash Morse code. The bulletin was the first word of the battle to reach the world, eleven days after it was fought. Editor and telegrapher worked steadily for twenty-four hours, pouring out a 15,000-word story.

Captain Marsh meanwhile rounded up his crew and piloted the *Far West* across the river to Fort Abraham Lincoln, where at dawn Army officers informed Mrs. Custer and other waiting wives of their husbands' deaths.

Sioux Indians being transported to the Standing Rock Indian Agency line the upper decks of the steamboat Helena *about 1880. Army efforts after Custer's defeat forced the Sioux onto reservations.*

Although the Sioux had triumphed and shocked the United States, their victory did not last long. Under pressure from other Army forces, they scattered, were defeated bit by bit, and returned to their reservations. Soon men, women, and children traveled up the rivers in peace to develop ranches and farms on the former hunting grounds of the Sioux.

CHAPTER TWELVE

By Night and by Day

CAPTAIN Ned Wakeman felt a surge of pride when he looked at his splendid new steamboat in the New York City shipyard where she had just been built. And well he should. The sparkling *New World* was a beauty. She had been constructed on luxurious lines, to carry passengers along the Hudson River between New York City and Albany. She was 225 feet long, with her name printed in bold letters on the wooden casings that covered her high, splashing side wheels. Crystal chandeliers and gilt mirrors adorned her elegant cabin, and she was expected to speed at almost twenty miles an hour, very fast for a steamboat in 1850.

But alas for Captain Wakeman. It looked as though he never would be able to stand at the front of the *New World*'s upper deck, dressed impressively in his blue uniform with gold decorations, and ring the sailing bell. The owner had spent more money to build the steamboat than he possessed or could borrow. Those to whom he owed money complained to a judge, who put deputy sheriffs aboard with orders to prevent Captain Wakeman from taking the boat from the shipyard until the debts were paid.

Instead of acting angrily toward these officers of the law, the sly captain treated them like honored guests. He gave them much to eat and even more to drink. When everyone was being congenial and jovial, he suggested that if the *New World* must be sold to pay the owner's debts, she would be worth more to potential buyers if a test run had demonstrated how fast she was.

"Let me take her on a trip down the harbor and back," he suggested to the sheriff's men. In their relaxed mood, that sounded reasonable to them and they agreed.

They didn't know, however, that the captain had secretly been storing fuel and provisions for a long voyage aboard the *New World*.

Down the Hudson past Manhattan Island the *New World* steamed. The deputies admired her speed and smooth performance. However, when Captain Wakeman kept the boat sailing out toward the Atlantic Ocean, instead of turning back, they began to feel uneasy. At the Narrows, between Brooklyn and Staten Island, Captain Wakeman stopped the boat.

He said to the deputy sheriffs, "Do you want to go to California with us? Or would you prefer to go ashore here?"

The sheepish deputies chose to land and were rowed ashore. While they went home reluctantly to confess how they had been tricked, the captain took the *New World*, which had been built to sail on a quiet river, out into the turbulent Atlantic and turned her toward South America. Profitable as sailing up and down the Hudson would have been, he knew that out in California the Gold Rush beckoned.

From New York to San Francisco by sea around the tip of South America, and then back up the west coast of Mexico and the United States, was a journey of fifteen thousand miles. Hugging the shore as much as she could, but buffeted by storms, the adventurous riverboat worked her way down the South American coast. Her side wheels churned the long saltwater swells of the Atlantic, and she proved to be sturdy.

At Rio de Janeiro, Brazil, a British frigate forced the *New World* into port because she didn't have proper sailing papers. But ingenious Captain Wakeman was equal to the situation. He "accidentally" fell overboard from a small boat in the harbor and

The adventurous New World, which made the trip around Cape Horn from New York to San Francisco, was not a streamlined ocean liner but a riverboat.

Mid-nineteenth century map of New York City shows the Narrows between Brooklyn and Staten Island.

The New World ended up as a ferryboat on San Francisco Bay.

convinced the American consul that he had lost the vessel's papers while struggling in the water. A tragic catastrophe befell the *New World*, too. A yellow fever epidemic killed eighteen of her crewmen. But onward she sailed.

Weeks after rounding Cape Horn and turning north in the Pacific Ocean, the *New World* reached the Isthmus of Panama, only to find process servers waiting to collect the owner's debts. She also found gold-hungry Forty-Niners, anxious for a ride to San Francisco on any ship that came along. The high fares they were willing to pay were enough for the captain to settle the debts. Once more Wakeman got the *New World* out to sea, and on to San Francisco.

In her new home on the West Coast, she became a riverboat, as originally intended, hailed as the speed and luxury queen of the Sacramento River between Sacramento and San Francisco. Sometimes on down-river trips she carried gold dust worth hundreds of thousands of dollars in her safe. Passengers going upstream through the California plains included men on their way to the gold fields, intent on getting rich. On her return trips she carried a few miners who had done so, as well as hundreds who were going home in disgust, almost empty handed. Later the *New World* served as a passenger packet on the Columbia River. In her old age, she became a ferryboat on San Francisco Bay, carrying commuters to their jobs from suburban waterside towns.

The Hudson River trade, from which the *New World* had been so daringly snatched, was less adventurous than the boat's assignments in the West but nevertheless was traditionally among the most glamorous steamboat routes in the country. From the time of Robert Fulton's *Clermont* until the late 1930s when scheduled passenger service ceased, the Albany day and night boats were a popular way to travel. Many boys and girls, and their parents too, had their first experience of riding on water aboard the Hudson River steamers.

At first, these Hudson River steamboats were small, but they were replaced by large vessels more like ocean-going ships than like the Mississippi River boats. Fulton set strict rules for passengers on his Hudson River steamboats. Some of these were:

"According to the order in which passengers pay their fares, they will be entitled to entry into the washroom. . . . It is not permitted that any person shall smoke in the ladies cabin, or in the

Two views of the Hudson River and the Palisades. One, RIGHT, shows the first steamboat, the Clermont; *in the other, a later and more elegant steamboat plies the Hudson from New York City to Albany.*

great cabin, under the penalty, first, of one dollar and a half, and a half a dollar for each half hour they offend against the rule; the money to be spent in wine for the company. It is not permitted for any person to lie down in a berth with their boots or shoes on. . . . In the ladies cabin, and in the great cabin, cards and all other games are to cease at ten o'clock at night, that those persons who wish to sleep may not be disturbed."

A British traveler on the river in those early days told how special consideration was given to women.

"No man is admitted into the dining saloon until all the ladies are seated at the table, when they rush in pellmell. After that should a lady require either, the chair is, without ceremony, taken from under you and the plate from before you. . . . It seemed to me that women were treated like petted children and that they must often feel rather annoyed by the excessive politeness and consideration shown them. At the same time it is an honor of this country that an unprotected woman of any age may travel through its length and breadth . . . without insult or the slightest attempt to take advantage of her youth or inexperience."

A writer for Frank Leslie's *Popular Monthly* traveled on the New York-to-Albany day boat in 1882 and in an article reported the scenic beauties of the day-long journey. He also described humorously his eight or nine hundred fellow passengers, giving us a glimpse of how traveling Americans looked a hundred years ago.

"A joyous, bustling, expectant, excited, well-bred, fashionable crowd buzzes around the decks," he wrote. "Old ladies, young ladies, middle-age ladies, and ladies of no particular age at all, attired in traveling costumes of every conceivable sort, shape, size, and description. . . . Some wear linen dusters from chin to heel, until they look as though attired for a sack race. Hats! . . . such grace, such elegance, such sweep, such *chic*, such loveliness, such head-caressers!"

The elaborate hair-dos of the women aboard astonished him. "Hair! Ye gods! black, brown, chestnut, auburn, wine-colored, red, yellow and white; in plaits, pigtails, curls, corkscrews, bands, kisses,

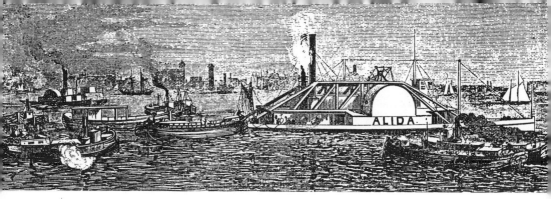

View of shipping in busy New York Harbor

Montagues, shells, rolls, and every other form known to the advanced females of this the fag end of the nineteenth century. . . ."

Undoubtedly this shipboard reporter exaggerated what he had seen, but not by very much. The bulky and intricate costumes women wore in the 1880s, even on a shipboard vacation, were formidable.

Then he looked at the male passengers. "Old dandies, with dyed hair and side-whiskers . . . portly brokers in stiff white waistcoats . . . languid swells in blue shirts, with striped stockings and patent-leather shoes.

"Little groups soon form themselves. . . . The bows are extensively patronized, camp stools in tremendous requisition. . . . Jaunty young gentlemen, with a view to exhibit their intrepidity, sit loosely on the bulwarks, allowing their feet to hang over the side of the ship, to the admiration and dismay of the young ladies. . . . In the remotest corners of the boat sit the brand-new brides and bridegrooms."

In those days, travelers did not enjoy the loose comfort of open-necked sports shirts and similar casual clothing. Men wore stiff collars, neckties, and hats even while on excursion trips. No young woman would have dreamed of appearing in slacks, had such garb existed. Or even worse, shorts! A shock wave of furious condemnation would have swept through the other feminine passengers. No matter how hot the weather, all women wore full, heavy skirts that swept the decks. Often they fastened their hats with scarves tied under the chin to prevent them from blowing overboard.

An excursion steamer, paddle wheels churning, flags flying

Overnight trips by passenger steamer along the bays and rivers of the East Coast, and between Los Angeles and San Francisco on the West Coast, were a luxurious and leisurely way to travel. One popular route was from New York to Boston, another was the night boat between New York and Albany, and a third was along Chesapeake Bay between Baltimore and Norfolk, Virginia.

These night boats sailed about 5:00 P.M. Passengers had an excellent dinner aboard, strolled on the deck or sat in the spacious lounge during the evening, then retired to their cabins to sleep. The motion of the water was soothing, a gentle rocking, not like the heavy rolling and pitching that passengers had to endure on trips across the Atlantic. The next morning the boat either docked before breakfast or offered a generous breakfast aboard, depending upon the length of the run. Boats of one famous company, the Fall River Line, docked at Fall River, Massachusetts, from New York before dawn; the passengers had to rise early and walk from the ship to a train waiting alongside the dock at 6:00 A.M. They rode the rest of the way to Boston by rail, arriving at 7:30 A.M.

Vessels on these coastal night runs resembled small ocean liners in several respects. Some had screw propellers, others side paddle wheels. The most elaborate ones were three or four decks tall and had iron hulls designed for deep water. Ornate grand staircases led from the main decks up to the main cabins. A few carried a thousand or more passengers. When two of these large night boats, brilliantly illuminated, passed each other in Long Island Sound on a starry night, the scene was one long to be remembered by the passengers. Some of the largest passenger ships on the Great Lakes, running along Lake Erie between Detroit and Buffalo, were similar in size and accommodations to the finest coastal night boats.

Out on the Pacific Coast, steamboat passengers dressed and behaved less fashionably than those back East. Most of them were more concerned with getting rich in the mines or making a living in the raw new towns than with showing off their social graces. Fast passenger steamboats sailed on the great waterways of the West—Puget Sound in the Pacific Northwest; the Columbia River and its long, twisting tributary, the Snake, to the south; and farther down the coast, the network of waterways leading inland from

Steamer travel was very popular in the late 1900s. There were day and night lines from New York to nearby cities. Pictured here, LEFT, is the Puritan (1889), a passenger boat of the Fall River Line, which traveled between New York and Boston. RIGHT: A view of the New York waterfront showing Albany day and night line and excursion steamers at the docks.

San Francisco Bay. Among the busiest vessels were those on the Sacramento River to Sacramento, the jumping-off place for the Forty-Nine gold rush into the mountains beyond.

In these regions, the boats sailed partially on tidal saltwater from the Pacific Ocean. While these vessels looked elegant to travelers not accustomed to luxuries in a pioneer land, their accommodations were less elaborate than those back East.

Although she was among the finest, the *New World* had a knack for getting into trouble in the West as well as in New York. Her reputation for speed and splendid food made other shipowners jealous, and the company that operated her was unpopular, being regarded by many as a monopoly. The citizens of Benicia, a river town, sponsored a rival boat, the *Washoe*. The two boats competed one day to reach the landing at Benicia. Although the *New World* pulled in first, the wharf crew refused to handle her lines and she had to back out into the stream. Up puffed the *Washoe*, cut across the *New World*'s bow, and glided in to the landing.

"He can't get away with that!" the *New World*'s pilot exclaimed.

Angrily he rang the signal for full speed ahead and drove the *New World* hard into the side of the *Washoe*, which wallowed toward shore and sank. One passenger on the *Washoe* was killed by flying debris.

Efforts by Benicia officials to prosecute the *New World*'s pilot failed, but thereafter the boat was an uneasy and not very welcome guest at the port.

Among the renowned steamboats on the Columbia River was the sleek, slim *Telephone*, the fastest vessel ever to travel that stream. When the first steamboat in Oregon, the *Columbia*, sailed between Astoria and Portland in 1850, she needed twenty-seven hours for the journey of almost a hundred miles. The *Telephone* made the same run thirty years later in a little more than five hours. Even after a fire that almost destroyed her, the *Telephone* kept her speed. This happened as she approached the dock at Astoria. Flames flashed up from her boiler room and spread through the decks. Acting quickly, Captain U. B. Scott drove the vessel ashore at

Old print of Astoria, Oregon, terminus of a steamboat run

twenty miles an hour. Although the passengers and crewmen
jumped from her lower deck to safety on the riverbank, Captain
Scott found himself trapped in the pilothouse atop the vessel. Behind him, the ladders had burned. The captain made a desperate
but not very graceful dive out the pilothouse window into the
river and escaped alive.

Like numerous other coastal and river steamers, the *Telephone*
eventually became a ferryboat on San Francisco Bay, making frequent trips daily between San Francisco and Oakland. Her speed
remained so good that she regularly outran another specially built
ferryboat on the same run, to the cheers of her passengers.

Keeping track of which steamboat was which wasn't always easy,
especially in the West. Boats were sold, or rebuilt after sinking,
and put back into operation under a different name. Engines and
other parts were salvaged from one boat and installed on another.
A vessel widely known on the Columbia River as the *Lot Whit-
comb* showed up later on the Sacramento as the *Annie Abernathy*.

Another steamboat on the upper Columbia started life as the *Flint*. After she sank, the craft was brought to the surface, repaired, and sailed again as the *Fashion*, powered by engines salvaged from the abandoned *Columbia*.

Nobody ever had any questions about the tough old *Eliza Anderson*, however. Everybody on Pacific Northwest waters knew her. She was slow but rugged, sailing on various waterways for forty years during which she became a competitor in wars between shipowners over fares and routes. For awhile she fought with the rival side-wheeler *Enterprise* for passengers and cargo along Puget Sound. Tiring of having to cut shipping rates to get business, the owners of the *Enterprise* took her out of service, whereupon the owners of the *Eliza Anderson* purchased her engine and installed it in their boat. Strengthened and speeded up by this "heart transplant," the *Eliza Anderson* sailed on into further adventures.

Rival owners put a faster side-wheeler, the *George E. Starr*, into service on the same route up to Victoria, British Columbia, against *Eliza*. The *Starr* played a game that infuriated the *Eliza Anderson*'s crew. The *Starr* ran alongside the aging old lady wherever she sailed; as they approached each port, the *Starr* turned on her superior speed and pulled into dock ahead of the *Eliza Anderson*, hoping to attract passengers who might otherwise have taken passage on her.

Ownerships changed, but the *Eliza Anderson*'s crew didn't forget this humiliation. One gloomy night the two steamers were running on almost parallel courses as they entered a heavy bank of fog that had settled over the Sound. Only one of them emerged from the fog: the *Eliza Anderson*. In the murky darkness she had turned her bow into the side of the *George E. Starr* and nearly demolished her hated rival. While the *Eliza Anderson* steamed on her way, the *George E. Starr* had to summon help and was towed into Seattle for repairs. The owners of the *Starr* claimed that the *Eliza*'s captain had attacked their vessel intentionally, for revenge. Pleading innocence, the captain contended that the collision was an accident. In that blinding fog, who could determine what the truth was?

City of Seattle, *old passenger steamer on the Alaska run*

When the gold rush to Alaska occurred in 1897, the *Eliza Anderson* creaked with age. Her engine had lost most of its power and she looked as though she belonged on the junk heap. But hundreds of men clamored for ship passage to Alaska, so old *Eliza* put out to sea in the Pacific with eighty-six gold-hungry passengers. The trip was a nightmare for them. Her engine broke down. She ran out of coal. The passengers had to help the crew bail out to keep afloat. When the *Eliza Anderson* finally crept into Dutch Harbor, the passengers refused to go any farther aboard her. She was abandoned at anchor in the harbor; a few months later her anchor chain snapped in a storm and she was blown onto shore with several holes torn in her bottom. There she slowly fell to pieces.

CHAPTER THIRTEEN

Sandbars, Beavers, and Mosquitoes

STEAMBOATS known more for durability than beauty, and for captains who would try almost anything to make a profit, nosed up rivers from the west and southwest coasts of the United States in the late 1800s and early 1900s. Poor country cousins of the big-river passenger packets, they usually needed paint and often lacked such niceties as deck rails and comfortable cabin accommodations. They hauled passengers and cargo to remote communities. Odd things often happened to them.

Communities of early settlers along Puget Sound in the Pacific Northwest found themselves isolated on its numerous inlets and islands because so few roads existed. They needed the Puget Sound "mosquito fleet" of small steamboats that chugged from settlement to settlement. Service was so informal that captains of these little rag-tag vessels often picked up grocery shopping lists from farm wives along the shore, purchased groceries for them in town, and delivered the packages on the steamer's homeward trip.

Often farmers shipped their livestock by steamboat along with their produce. Having pigs and horses aboard gave a boat a certain air of informality, and a barnyard stench, too. The small-river steamboats were workhorses, hauling anything for a fee and willing

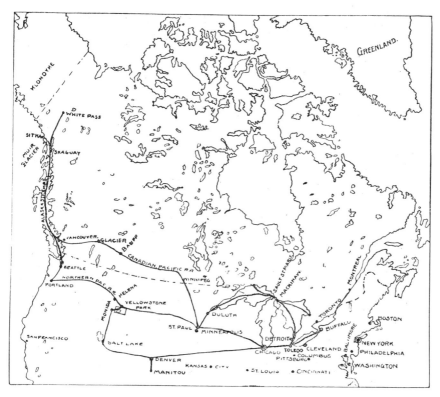

An old tour map of Puget Sound trip to Alaska

to nose ashore for a "mud landing" to take aboard a load whenever someone set up a signal flag.

In Oregon one day, the steamboat *Chester* was carrying such cargo from ranch to ranch along the Cowlitz River. On her forward deck, the *Chester* had a pen in which was contained a pig being shipped to a new owner. Somehow the pig broke loose. Deckhands gave chase. Squirming past them, the pig jumped overboard and swam toward shore. The deckhands plunged into the river in pursuit. They chased the pig into a field and thought they had it cornered, only to see the farmer's angry bull trotting toward them. Back they scurried to the safety of the boat. The liberated pig was left to run loose until the *Chester* came past the field on a later trip; then her crewmen, after making sure that the bull wasn't in sight, recaptured the porker and delivered it to its proper destination.

Then there was the dingy *Mud Hen*, which was just about as small as a steamboat could be. Tiny as she was, just thirty-two feet long and six feet wide, the little stern-wheeler served her public faithfully if not swiftly on the Coquille River of Oregon. The *Mud Hen* was only a few inches narrower than Beaver Slough, an arm of the Coquille on which she sailed. Shrubbery hung over the banks of the slough and trees formed an archway above its five-mile length from the Coquille to the small community of Toledo. That was the *Mud Hen*'s daily route.

She had a vexing navigational problem of a kind never faced by bigger and finer craft: beavers. Happy and busy among all those trees, each night the beavers built dams across Beaver Slough. Each morning the *Mud Hen*'s two-man crew pulled on high gumboots and tore down the dams so their boat could sail.

Once when the water level in Beaver Slough was so low that even the flat-bottomed *Mud Hen* could barely navigate, a passenger remarked, "What you need are locks instead of dams."

A regular passenger on the *Mud Hen*, a man quick with a pun, replied, "Don't mention it. There are locks of my hair on every

The little steamboat Mud Hen *was beset by a unique problem. Each night the busy beavers of Oregon built dams across streams on her route.*

Captain Minnie Hill

crabapple tree between the Coquille and Toledo."

In those days, when women didn't even have the right to vote, steamboating was a man's business. Women worked aboard as cabin stewardesses and sometimes as cooks, but that was about all. Rarely there was an exception, when a determined woman with luck on her side became a steamboat captain. Among the best known was Captain Minnie Hill of the Columbia River.

When she was twenty, Minnie married a steamboat captain, Charles Hill. That was in 1883. The bride spent many days in the pilothouse with her husband; he taught her about the river's tricky currents and the job of piloting. Three years later, she had learned so much that she passed the required examination and became the first licensed female steamboat pilot west of the Mississippi. After another three years, the Hills bought a good-sized stern-wheeler, the *Governor Newell*, 112 feet long, and operated it as a freight-hauler under an unusual arrangement. Captain Minnie commanded the boat, presiding over its big wheel in the pilothouse, while her husband, Captain Charles, went below to the engine room and worked as her chief engineer. She gave the signals, and he made the engines do what she ordered.

Captain Minnie not only ran the boat; she was a mother at the same time. She had a baby son, and the family lived aboard the *Governor Newell* for a number of years, meanwhile acquiring four more boats. Even after she established a home on shore so their son could go to school, Captain Minnie often commanded a Hill boat when the company needed a fill-in captain. That was a century ago. If the Hills were sailing today under such an arrangement, the feminist movement probably would give Captain Charles an award for promoting equal rights for women. Not merely equal rights, in fact, but superior rights, since Minnie had learned about steamboating from him.

Around on the southwestern coast of the United States, in Texas and New Mexico, the Rio Grande is a famous river. Country and western musicians sing about it. Wagon-train parties felt as though they had really reached the West when they crossed it. But along much of its length, the stream didn't live up to its name "Grande." Steamboat captains coaxed and nudged their vessels about six hundred miles up from its mouth to Laredo, but no farther. Early in the 1900s, steamboats quit running on the river.

Last of the Rio Grande boats was a tiny low-powered stern-wheeler, the *Bessie*, best known for her habit of running backward. Often when the *Bessie* came to a bend, the roaring Texas wind pushed her stern around in an arc while her bow stuck on the bank. The current broke her loose, and she proceeded downstream tail first. At the next big bend, the captain steered the stern into the bank and waited while wind and current pushed her nose around to the front again. Away went the *Bessie* downstream, headed forward in the normal way. A passenger who endured these back-and-front antics reported "and so she waltzed us all the way to Brownsville."

At least the *Bessie* kept moving. Steamboats that went up Texas rivers in the dry season sometimes became trapped and had to wait for months until autumn rains filled the channel. When that happened to one boat, its enterprising crew planted cotton in a field nearby, tended it through the summer, harvested it, and carried the crop down to market when their boat finally floated free.

Of all the rivers in the United States on which steamboats ventured, the nastiest sailing anywhere was on the lonely Colorado River, which along much of its length forms the boundary between California and Arizona.

Except during the spring runoff season from mountain snows, the Colorado's shallow bottom was riddled with sandbars. Even though the boats that sailed on the river drew only two feet of water, they became stuck constantly. Even worse, the Colorado flows through hundreds of miles of desolate, barren desert and rocky canyons, so hot in summer that temperatures between 110 and 120 degrees Fahrenheit in the shade are commonplace—and rarely is shade to be found. Chuffing slowly up the river on a dingy steamboat with primitive accommodations was a test of endurance for passengers and crewmen. It was like living in an oven with the gas turned high. The sun beat down relentlessly. There was a frequently told joke at the time about a soldier stationed at the Yuma crossing of the Colorado who died and went to hell, then sent back for his blankets because the weather there was so cold compared to Yuma.

Add to that the night-time torture of mosquitoes. When a Colorado steamboat tied up to the shore at dusk, the buzzing, hungry insects swarmed around it in masses. Passengers had to choose between trying to sleep on hard straw mattresses in their sweltering boxlike wooden cabins or putting their mattresses on deck, where a breeze might stir. After a night on deck, most passengers preferred their cabins as the lesser misery. This description of a Colorado steamboat watchman dressed to protect himself

Map shows the long twisting course of the Colorado River.

against mosquitoes, published in the Yuma *Sentinel*, gives an idea of what Colorado River night life was like:

"He wore close-fitting canvas trousers and jacket, fisherman's boots, a wire helmet and masque covered with fine gauze and buckskin gauntlets. In the sole of each boot was a hole plugged with a cork. When the inside man felt that his boots were about full of perspiration, he pulled the corks."

In summer, when the heat was almost intolerable, women passengers complained that the sizzling galvanized iron plates on the decks burned their feet through the soles of their shoes. When the passengers ate, the knives and forks were so hot the people could barely touch them. Sandstorms swirling across the desert cut visibility to zero and covered boat and passengers with a bone-dry, gritty layer of dust that sifted through clothing and into every little crevice.

Just getting a steamboat into the waters of the Colorado was an ordeal. No materials for boatbuilding existed within two hundred miles of the river. Only skimpy supplies could be brought by mule across the sand dunes from the west to Fort Yuma. The fort stood at the point where the southern pioneer trail crossed the river about seventy-five miles north of its mouth on the Gulf of California. Below Yuma, the Colorado was so shallow and twisting that its channel meandered 150 miles to cover the 75-mile distance. Early steamboats struggling up to Yuma from the gulf needed as much as two weeks to travel that stretch. Desolate mud flats spread out from the river on both sides. Few places in North America were so dreary.

A woman who came ashore near the Colorado's mouth wrote of it: "Just imagine a place where there is not a tree nor a stone as large as a pea, not a bit of anything green as far as the eye can reach, excepting a little salt grass along the very edge of the river." Another said in a diary: "The wind was like the breath from a furnace."

The usual way to get a steamboat onto the Colorado was for an ocean vessel to unload sections of the riverboat at the mouth of the river, where they were assembled.

This unloading was complicated by a tremendous tidal bore, a wall of saltwater that surged from the often rough Gulf of California across the mudflats and raced several miles up the river channel. Ocean steamers often waited several days for the waters to calm enough for them to put their cargo ashore.

Although a handful of dingy steamboats made the trip as far as Fort Yuma in the early 1850s, almost nothing was known about the river north of the fort. The Colorado flows westward through the mountains of northern Arizona, forming the magnificent Grand Canyon for a long distance, then emerges through other narrow, spectacular gorges and flows south through the desert to Yuma. The Army in Washington needed to know how far upstream steamboats could go, so in 1857 it ordered Lieutenant Joseph Christmas Ives to find out. Ives and his party of scientists had a voyage they long remembered.

First, they needed a boat. Ives had the *Explorer*, a little iron-hulled stern-wheeler just fifty-four feet long, built at Philadelphia, tested, and then dismantled into eight sections. These were carried aboard an Atlantic Ocean vessel south to Panama, hauled across the tropical isthmus, and shipped north on a Pacific steamship to San Francisco. There, the *Explorer*'s sections were placed aboard a sailing ship, which hauled them south again on a month-long trip around the tip of Baja California and up the Gulf of California to the mouth of the Colorado River, a total distance of some seventeen thousand miles.

Assembling the *Explorer* was tedious and difficult. Using logs hauled two miles across the mudflats, the crew built a wooden runway in a long trench, on which they put together the parts. Nearly a month passed before the *Explorer* was a whole boat able to get up steam for her voyage. With the desert sun gleaming on her bright red paint, the little craft started for Yuma. Since her cabin was only a box, eight by seven feet, the crew slept ashore each night.

Early in January, 1858, Lieutenant Ives gave the command for the *Explorer* to depart upstream from Yuma. As her smokestack poured out a black cloud from the cottonwood logs she burned, the vessel pulled out from Fort Yuma to the cheers and shouts of the garrison. Away she sailed—but not far. While still within view of the fort, the *Explorer* ran aground. That was only the beginning. The little steamer seemed to pass more time stuck in the sand than afloat. At one point she spent three days moving nine miles.

The Indians along the river thought that watching the white man's fire-eating monster get stuck was hilarious. As Ives said in his official report, they laughed with "unqualified delight" at his

Compared to rugged conditions in the West, steamboat travel in the East seemed almost to be a picnic. Here a hunter shoots at ducks from the deck of a small rustic steamboat as it chugs through the wilderness on the Magalloway River in Maine. The women in the center and along the left rail of the vessel hardly seem dressed for a hunting expedition.

boat's woes. The Indians gathered to watch the show wherever they knew there was a sandbar. Seeing a group of Indians ahead caused the crew of the *Explorer* to let out loud moans; they knew this as a sure sign of trouble lurking.

Farther upstream, the Mojave Indians came to pay a call on the steamboat. Cairook, the chief, rode out to the vessel on a raft towed by a team of swimmers. Ives made a speech of welcome, then took the chief and his grass-skirted squaw for a short ride on the steamboat—thereby, Ives reported, probably raising her social status among the Indian women immensely.

Finally, in Black Canyon about four hundred miles north of Yuma, the *Explorer* hit a rock so hard that Ives decided she had reached the highest point of navigable water on the Colorado. This point is a short distance below where the massive Hoover Dam blocks the river and forms Lake Mead today.

After the *Explorer* returned to Yuma, Ives sold her for one thousand dollars. She hauled freight on the river until a towering sandstorm tore her loose from her moorings at Yuma in the 1870s and she drifted downstream into a sandy morass, abandoned and forgotten. Thirty years ago, a party of searchers chopped their way with machetes through thickets of arrowweed along the riverbank, hoping to find the remnants of the historic boat and bring them back to a museum. They found the wreckage, after much searching, but were too late. Decades of relentless sun and sandstorms had caused it to deteriorate so badly that the iron remnants had rusted into brittle fragments too fragile to move. What is left of the *Explorer*, if anything, still lies in the jungle of tall, dank weeds. The river has changed course so much that the boat's last resting place may not even be near the water any longer.

Since travel on the Colorado was so miserable, why did people bother? Lieutenant Ives, for one, didn't see much sense in it. In his report he wrote, "The region . . . is, of course, altogether valueless. After entering it there is nothing to do but leave. Ours has been the first, and will doubtless be the last, party of whites to visit this profitless locality. It seems intended by nature that the Colorado River, along the greater portion of its lonely and majestic way, shall be forever unvisited and undisturbed."

What a bad prediction that was!

Considerable steamboat traffic developed after the *Explorer*'s trip because the river was the easiest way to reach the mining camps that sprang up in the desert mountains and the Army posts that

174

were built to protect them. Roads in the desert were almost non-existent. The boats carried soldiers, civilians, and supplies to these outposts. Often they towed barges to increase their cargo capacity.

Conditions never improved much for the steamboats, however. The diary of a passenger who traveled up the river in the stern-wheeler *Cocopah* in 1878 is full of such entries as: "Stuck, four miles farther on. The captain gets into a boat to take soundings for passage. . . . Here we are stuck again. We spend two hours before finding a passage deep enough to continue. . . . We are stuck but get off rather quickly. . . . The two Indians we saw running were scouts who announced our arrival to their village hidden behind the cottonwoods."

Steamboats quit running on the Colorado below Yuma after the Southern Pacific Railroad built its track across the desert, intersecting the river at Yuma. Today they couldn't sail on the lower Colorado even if they were needed. About seventy-five years ago, river waters burst through the western bank below Yuma and poured across the desert to form the Salton Sea in a desert valley that is below sea level. After three years, the river was conquered and returned to its course. Meanwhile, so much silt had drifted and been blown into the riverbed that the waters had no clearly defined channel, just a number of small shifting ones. Since then, construction of dams and irrigation projects along its course has reduced the "mighty" Colorado River's flow so much that near its mouth the river narrows into a channel through the mud flats so small during much of the year that a man can almost step across it.

CHAPTER FOURTEEN

Today's Bustling Waterways

AT the end of a steamboat trip, the final signal the pilot telegraphed to the engine room was, "Finished with engines." By the close of the 1800s and the early 1900s, that signal came to mean not merely the completion of a routine trip but the end of a boat's life. The vessel was taken out of service and either abandoned to rot at an anchorage or towed to a shipyard for junk. The fascinating days of steamboating were ending, just as the canalboat era had ended earlier. Steamboats disappeared from the rivers and lakes because they no longer were needed.

Faster ways of transporting passengers had arrived. First came the railroads. Whenever railroad tracks came to a river town, steamboats fell upon evil days. Trains were faster, although they often were less comfortable.

Then the automobile arrived. Early-day cars were faster than a horse, but American roads had been built for horses, not automobiles—dirt and gravel routes that were wallows of mud part of the time or dusty in the dry months. During the 1920s and 1930s, most main roads were paved with concrete or asphalt, and many new roads were constructed. Travel by automobile became faster and far more common. Large trucks began to haul freight that formerly went by railroad.

Finally, commercial aviation developed. Passengers flew from the

With her powerful stern paddle wheel churning the river water, the famous Delta Queen *carries a large party of tourists on a nostalgic voyage along the Ohio River, following the course of early-day steamboats.*

Atlantic Coast to the Pacific Coast in five or six hours, instead of riding three or four days on the train. Travel by highway for short distances and by air for long trips replaced railroad journeys. The automobile and the jetliner destroyed most passenger-train service, just as trains had eliminated steamboat and canalboat travel. Americans want to get there in a hurry.

Yet by rushing at such a headlong pace, we have lost something from life that our forefathers had, a comfortable sense of leisurely progress. Eating dinner in the spacious dining room of a Great Lakes steamer or a Mississippi River packet while the scenery slipped past was more relaxing than sitting strapped into a narrow airliner seat, eating heated-up food from a tray balanced on the lap.

Delta Queen's *forward cabin lounge*

Sensing that the old ways had certain desirable elements our sleek, plastic, electronic life-style lacks, people try to recapture them through forms of nostalgia. One of these searches for the past is riding aboard the *Delta Queen* and the *Mississippi Queen* on the Mississippi and Ohio rivers. As the only remaining overnight river passenger boats in operation, they attract thousands of cruise travelers each year.

The *Delta Queen* still sails only because Congress passed a special act in her favor. She began life in 1926 as a night boat between San Francisco and Sacramento. When that service shut down, she was sold to a new owner who had her towed through the Panama Canal and up to New Orleans. She is 285 feet long, with a steel hull and a partly wooden superstructure. When rigid new fire-safety rules for shipping passed by Congress in 1966 forbade wooden superstructures on large vessels, it appeared that the *Delta Queen* might be doomed. An outcry arose against destroying this last remnant of steamboating days, so every three years since then Congress has passed special legislation that exempts the *Delta Queen*. The boat has been rebuilt extensively to include additional safety factors and finer accommodations.

So many cruise passengers wanted to enjoy a taste of the past that the *Delta Queen*'s company in 1976 added a much larger new boat, the *Mississippi Queen*. Although built in a tall style reminiscent of the old Mississippi packets, the *Mississippi Queen* really is an elaborate modern floating hotel, 382 feet long and 68 feet wide. The two boats offer cruises of differing lengths on the Ohio and Mississippi.

Another way to taste the flavor of inland water travel is aboard the train ferry boats that sail across Lake Michigan from Ludington, Michigan, to Milwaukee. These large steel ferries carry freight cars, automobiles, and passengers. When seated in a sunny deck chair near the bow of a train ferry, out in the center of Lake Michigan, a passenger can easily believe that he or she is on a liner far out in the ocean. It isn't easy to remember at such a moment that scores of other vessels, much more flimsily built and often underpowered, encountered tragedy while sailing in these same waters during the past 150 years and now lie at the bottom of the lake.

Although the canals that frontier settlers found so wonderful were abandoned even before steamboats were, and in most places cannot be seen, traces of these can be visited at a number of spots by those who wish to see how our ancestors traveled. The locks and ditches look so small!

Motorists driving north on the New York State Thruway from Buffalo toward Niagara Falls don't realize it, but they are traveling directly above the bed of the original Erie Canal, which lies buried under concrete beneath the wheels of their automobiles.

The concept of the Erie Canal did not die out when the railroads and highways came, however. The route it followed across New York State was too important, even after the great westward rush of immigrant traffic died out. The Erie was rebuilt, enlarged, and slightly rerouted several times. Today its direct successor, the

Old photograph shows the Weighlock Building at Syracuse when it was a weigh station for canalboats, before it became the Canal Museum.

New York State Barge Canal, carries cargoes of bulk freight on barges pushed by diesel-powered towboats.

At Syracuse, New York, is the Canal Museum, housed in the Weighlock Building, a survivor from early canal days. It contained the scales that weighed passing canalboats to determine the tolls they must pay. Now it houses many exhibits illustrating life on the old canal. At Lockport, not far from Buffalo, visitors may take a guided tour of a section of the original canal, including the Five Flight Locks that lifted the boats up the high rocky escarpment there. And at Rome, close to the place where the first shovelful of dirt was turned for digging the long ditch, an Erie Canal Village has been reconstructed. Visitors see how people lived about 1840 and may ride aboard a horse-drawn passenger packet for a mile and a half of the original canal that has been restored. There are other parks, too, along the route of the original canal.

Those who wish to travel along the New York canal system, including portions of the original Erie, may do so aboard a double-decker steel powerboat, *Emita II*. Each summer *Emita II* makes trips of one to three days over canal sections between Albany and Buffalo, from her base at Syracuse, along with other trips.

A glimpse of frontier life as it was along the Ohio & Erie Canal is found at Roscoe Village, a restored canal town at Coshocton, Ohio. In addition to buildings, locks, and exhibits, a canalboat, the *Monticello II*, offers rides along a two-mile portion of the canal that has been restored.

On the great rivers where the smoke and whistles of steamboats once were commonplace—the Mississippi, the Ohio, the Missouri, and the Columbia—the waters still bustle with traffic. The commercial craft that cut through the currents today are immensely powerful diesel-powered tugboats pushing long lines of barges. Although lacking the glamour of the steamboats, these barges haul far more raw material for factories and foodstuffs for our tables than the old riverboats did.

Enormous sums of money have been spent to improve navigation conditions along the Mississippi. Captains of the towboats have navigational aids the steamboat captains never dreamed of: elec-

It is still possible to take a trip on a canal. The Emita II *travels the Erie, now the New York State Barge Canal. Pictured here, visitors at restored Roscoe Village enjoy a trip on the packet* Monticello II *behind hard-working horses on the Ohio & Erie towpath.*

tronic and telephone equipment on their craft, detailed weather and river condition reports, deep-dredged channels, and an abundance of buoys and lights to guide them. Nevertheless, danger lurks for them and their vessels in the fickle behavior of the river, just as it did for the steamboat pilots of Mark Twain's day. It just takes different forms.

A towboat on the Mississippi has three nine-foot propellers and pushes a line of barges a quarter-mile long. Keeping control of such a wiggly collection of rectangular objects lashed together requires close attention. At sharp turns in the river, the towboat must back up, then crawl forward, and repeat the maneuvers until it coaxes the elongated string of barges around the bend. A slight misjudgment in steering or in the amount of power applied will send the barges crashing into the shore. Since a towboat with loaded barges involves an investment of more than a million dollars, such accidents can be extremely costly. When a pilot loses control and the bulky barges turn sideways in the river, across the current, they become a hazard to shipping. They may smash into a bridge or hit other barge tows.

Going down the Mississippi from St. Louis to New Orleans under normal river conditions, a towboat shoving thirty loaded barges makes the trip in four and a half days. Upstream against the current, a big towboat can push forty-nine empty barges, fastened together like logs in a gigantic raft, seven long and seven abreast. The 1200-mile journey northbound usually takes ten days, compared to three days and eighteen hours the stripped-down *Robert E. Lee* required in its race against the *Natchez*. When headed upstream, tugboat pilots try to stay out of the main current and in the quieter water near shore, without running aground. Doing so requires a delicate hand at the controls.

In the words of a pilot whose upstream tow was caught in the fast-running main channel, "This is like pushing against a brick wall."

Dams built to collect water in reservoirs, from which it is carried by irrigation canals to farmlands, restrict barge traffic on the upper

Missouri River and on portions of other rivers where it might otherwise be possible. Reclamation projects are tremendously important. By distributing river water in this manner, the government has made it possible for thousands of otherwise dry acres to be cultivated. Much of the food on our tables comes from fields irrigated by river waters, which are spread in scientifically controlled flows. Electricity generated at dams provides power for homes, farms, and factories. Floods are prevented, too, by controlled release of water from the reservoirs. A system of dams and locks has created a controlled-depth waterway for barges on the Mississippi above St. Louis.

On the Great Lakes, although passenger steamers are just a memory, massive cargo boats, some a thousand feet long, plow through the water carrying immense loads of ore, grain, and other bulk commodities. Mingled with them are smaller, but still quite large, cargo ships from foreign countries hauling general freight deep into the heart of the United States and Canada. The flags of Great Britain, Norway, Sweden, Denmark, Poland, Japan, and

Tied up alongside the dock at Thunder Bay, Ontario, the Edward L. Ryerson *prepares to take aboard 27,000 tons of iron pellets in a nighttime loading operation.*

other countries fly from vessels tied up at wharfs in Great Lakes ports all the way from Duluth, Minnesota, to Toronto, Ontario. A person standing alongside the locks at Sault Ste. Marie can almost touch these carriers of the world's commerce, and of the wealth of our own mid-continent, and can greet sailors from foreign lands as they lean on the rails of their ships.

Come aboard one of these modern Great Lakes giants as she sails slowly out from a dock near Chicago, at the lower end of Lake Michigan, and heads northward. She has just delivered a load of 32,000 tons of iron ore from Minnesota. Now she is going back to Lake Superior for another load. Back and forth she goes, month after month, as monotonously as a city bus running its daily route. With engines that generate more than 7000 horsepower, the boat plows ahead, fair weather or foul.

From the high-rise cabin at her stern, a person looking forward sees hundreds and hundreds of feet of holds fastened shut with flat steel covers, an open stretch almost the length of three football fields. Over this expanse of steel, waves tumble one after another when a storm rakes the surface of the lakes. As the wind howls at fifty miles an hour, the deck almost disappears from view.

Crewmen and officers working on the deck communicate with the captain in his pilothouse by walkie-talkie radio. Almost everything is automated. When sailing in open water, the captain can turn on the automatic pilot. In the huge, glass-enclosed pilothouse an instrument panel flashes digital reports from a battery of instruments and measuring devices.

Despite these electronic controls, when the vessel enters narrow water approaching the locks at the Soo, the steersman at the controls and the officer in charge at the time must work with precision. The huge ore boat slows to less than ten miles an hour. As the officer issues oral orders—"Hard right . . . slower . . . faster now"— the vessel slides between the buoys marking the channel. Over the radio, instructions come from the superintendent of the locks on procedures for passing through. So much shipping uses this stair-step gateway between Lake Superior and the lower lakes that boats

The bulk cargo vessel Joseph L. Block *is so big and fast that she can carry three million tons of ore pellets annually from Lake Superior to other Great Lakes ports.*

often must wait their turn before they can enter the lock chamber to which they have been assigned. The most recently constructed lock at the Soo handles ships a thousand feet long. When an up-bound vessel is lifted from half concealment at the bottom of the lock to the higher, towering Lake Superior level, it appears gigantic, soaring over nearby buildings and spectators.

After passing through the lock, our vessel noses into Lake Superior and plods steadily the length of that extremely deep, often stormy, body of water until it reaches the ore port on the Minnesota shore at the lake's western end. Again guided by the captain's quick, precise orders, the vast bulk eases up to the dock, bumping the old tires that hang like cushions alongside. Crewmen throw ropes ashore, the deep hatches are uncovered, and soon ore pours down chutes into the hold. Barely twelve hours later, the whistle blasts its warning, lines are cast off, and, settling deep in the water, the boat departs toward the steel mills near Chicago, eight hundred miles away.

America's great waterways are hard at work. They serve lands populated by descendants of the pioneers who reached new homes on the frontier aboard the canalboats and the steamboats of an earlier century. Many of the rivers on which adventurous steamboat captains fought battles with sandbars now know only the roar of recreational powerboats. Water skiing has replaced "grasshoppering." But the lure of the water remains constant. If our ancestors hadn't had an overwhelming impulse to push west, and ingenuity to use the waterways as their roads into the wilderness, the America we know today would not have come into existence.

Bibliography

Research for a book of this nature involves examining many sources, some of them well known, others obscure. Those who wish to learn in more detail about specific aspects of canal life and steamboat days may do so from the following publications, which I found especially useful:

River Boats of America, by Frank Donovan (Thomas Y. Crowell, 1966)

Life on the Mississippi, by Mark Twain (Samuel Clemens)

The Steamboaters, by Harry Sinclair Drago (Dodd, Mead & Co., 1967)

American Notes, by Charles Dickens

Life on the River, by Norbury L. Wayman (Bonanza Books, 1971)

Water Trails West, a Western Writers of American anthology (Avon Books, 1978)

The Long Haul West, The Great Canal Era, 1817–1850, by Madeline Sadler Waggoner (G. P. Putnam's Sons, 1958)

Stars in the Water, The Story of the Erie Canal, by George E. Condon (Doubleday, 1974)

Canal Days in America, by Harry Sinclair Drago (Clarkson N. Potter, Inc., 1972)

The Erie Canal, Albany to Buffalo, by John P. Papp (John P. Papp Historical Publications, Schenectady, New York, 1977)

Erie Canal Days, A Pictorial Essay, Albany to Buffalo, by John P. Papp (John P. Papp Historical Publications, Schenectady, New York, 1975)

The Pageant of the Packets, by Garnett Laidlaw Eskew (Henry Holt & Co., 1929)

Transport to Disaster, by James W. Elliott (Holt, Rinehart and Winston, 1962)

Lloyd's Steamboat Directory and Disasters on the Western Waters, 1856, by James T. Lloyd (Lithographed by Young & Klein, Inc., Cincinnati, Ohio, 1979)

Mississippi Steamboatin', by Herbert E. Quick and Edward Quick (Henry Holt & Co., 1926)

River to the West, by Walter Havighurst (G. P. Putnam's Sons, 1970)

History of Early Steamboat Navigation on the Missouri River, by Hiram Martin Chittenden (F. P. Harper, 1903)

The Rivermen (Time-Life Books, 1975)

The Conquest of the Missouri, by Joseph Mills Hanson (A. C. McClurg, 1909)

Crazy Horse and Custer, by Stephan E. Ambrose (Doubleday, 1975)

Custer in '76, Walter Camp's Notes on the Custer Fight (Brigham Young University Press, 1976)

The Night Boat, by George W. Hilton (Howell-North Books, 1968)

Frank Leslie's Popular Monthly, August, 1882

Army Exploration in the American West, by William H. Goetzmann (Yale University Press, 1959)

Pacific Steamboats, by Gordon Howell and Joe Williamson (Superior Publishing Co., Seattle, 1958)

Blow for the Landing, by Fritz Timmen (Caxton Printers, 1973)

Index